Author: Adnan Morshed and Nesfun Nahar
Concept and Series Designer: Ariadna A. Garreta
Layout and Graphics Editor: Núria Sordé Orpinell

First Published, 2017

ISBN (Bloomsbury India) 978-93-87146-11-2

10 9 8 7 6 5 4 3 2 1

Printed and bound in India by Thomson Press India Ltd. 2017

Altrim Pubslishers
Passeig de Manuel Girona 55, baixos 2a
08034 Barcelona (Catalonia, Spain)
www.altrim.cat

in association with:

Bloomsbury Publishing India Pvt Limited
2nd Floor, LSC Building No. 4, DDA Complex
Pocket C 6&7, Vasant Kunj
New Delhi 110070 (India)
www.bloomsbury.com

Cover Photo: National Martyrs' Memorial (Jatiyo Smriti Shoudho) by Turjoy Chowdhury
Tower of Light (pp. 174–175) by Toh Yah Li

Published in India by Bloomsbury Publishing India Pvt Ltd on behalf of Altrim Publishers

altrim publishers

South Asia Architectural Travel Guides

ADNAN MORSHED & NESFUN NAHAR

DHAKA IN 25 BUILDINGS

BLOOMSBURY

NEW DELHI • LONDON • OXFORD • NEW YORK • SYDNEY

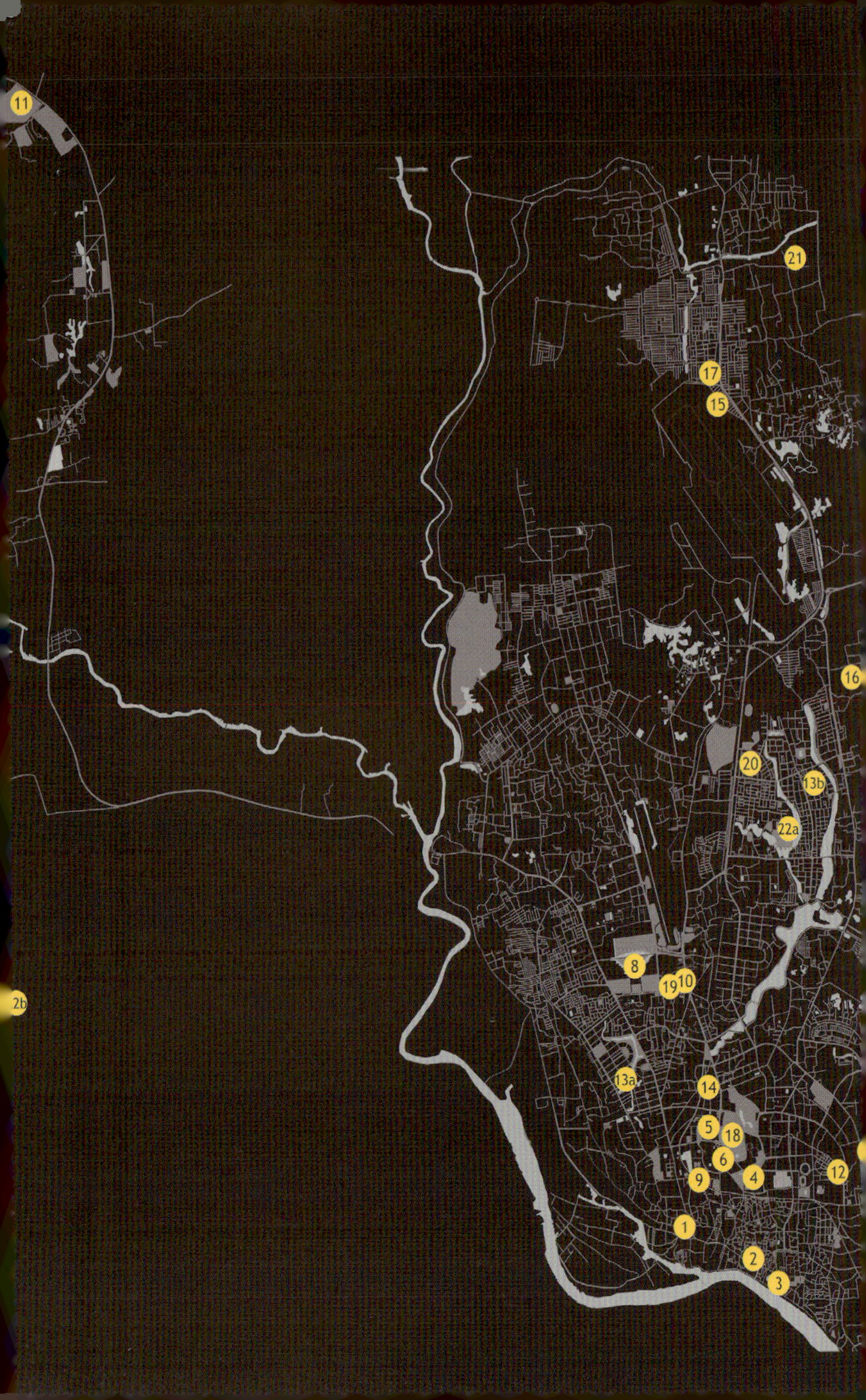
11
21
17
15
16
20
13b
22a
8
19
10
2b
13a
14
5
18
6
9
4
12
1
2
3

CONTENTS

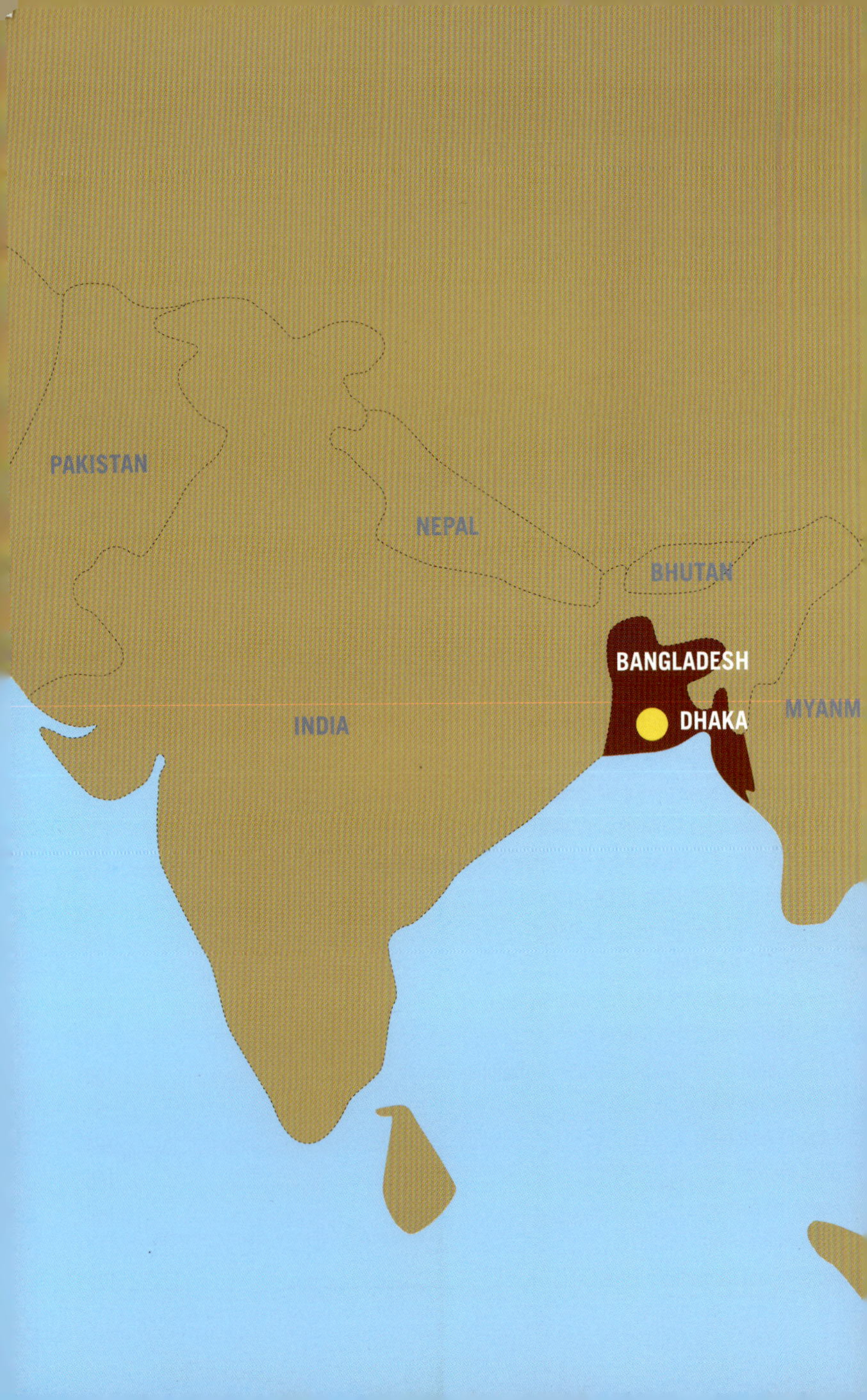
PAKISTAN
NEPAL
BHUTAN
BANGLADESH
DHAKA
INDIA
MYANM

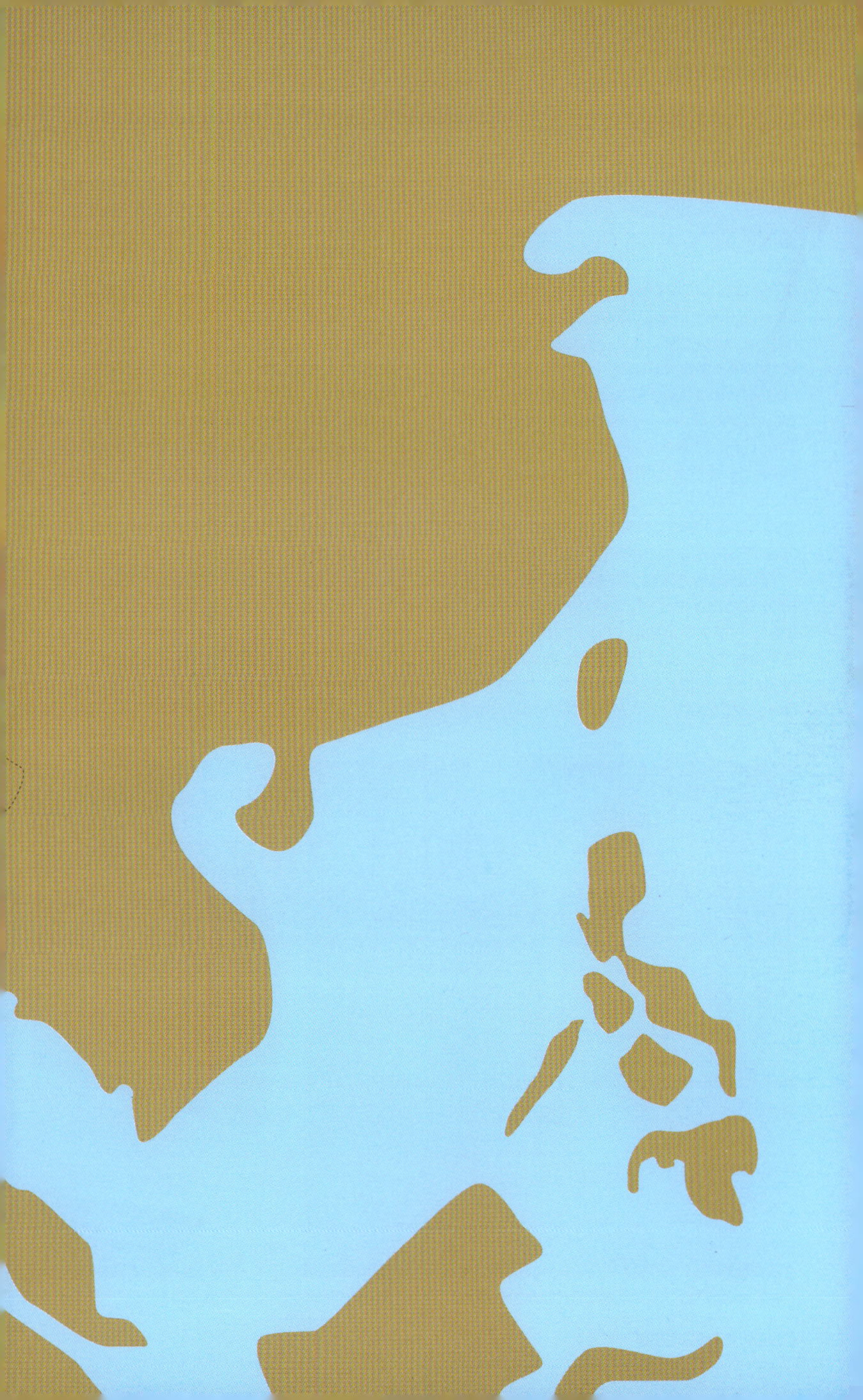

Dhaka: An Architectural Journey

Like other emerging megacities of the world, Dhaka has been growing exponentially, particularly since it became the capital of the independent nation of Bangladesh in 1971. Today, a visitor's first impression of this city could be bewildering. Streets swarm with pedestrians, rickshaws, motorbikes, cars, taxis, buses, and trucks. Vendors hawk virtually everything—from household goods to apparel to reprinted *New York Times* bestsellers. Enormous shopping arcades all across the city attract streams of consumers. Meanwhile, the Parliament building area, Ramna Park, and Hatir Jheel provide much-needed respite from the congestion and noise.

Multistory apartment buildings dominate the city's built environment, signaling the rise of an urban bourgeoisie. The impoverished but highly resilient slum city of Karail, in the shadow of the high-end Gulshan residential area, debunks the myth that urban poverty is seen only in the city's peripheral wasteland.

Dhaka is a quintessential 21st-century urban narrative of whirlwind modernity.

A Brief Historical Perspective

The provenance of the name Dhaka is obscure. (It was spelled Dacca until 1982; the airport code is still DAC.) Suggestions abound: the dak tree (butea frondosa), which once grew here abundantly; the Hindu Goddess Durga, found concealed in this location; the *dhak* (drum), beaten during Dhaka's inauguration as a provincial Mughal capital; a Prakrit dialect called Dhaka Bhasa; a *dhakka* (watch-station), as it was used in low flatlands; and Davaka, one of the administrative units of the Gupta Empire, when Gupta kings ruled over Samatata (eastern and southeastern Bengal), from the early 4th century CE to the late 6th century CE.

The National Assembly Building of Bangladesh (Jatiyo Shangshad Bhaban)

Independence Monument

Dhaka is a city with *history*. This South Asian metropolis, located at the geographic heart of a riverine delta, has been mentioned since ancient times. In *Oriental Commerce* (1813), William Milburn states that Roman historian Pliny the Younger observed the "presence of Dhaka's textiles in the Mediterranean trade as early as 73 [CE]." Dhaka enjoyed certain name recognition within the trading world of the Silk Road, as the city's famous muslin and fine embroidery were coveted in European royal courts, as much as they were in Sultani and Mughal royal circuits.

Most likely, Dhaka developed into a modest commercial hub during the era of the Sena rulers (c. 1097–1225). And, it held some significance under the independent Sultans of Bengal. Historians observe that the city was a revenue collection center during the reign of Sultan Barbak Shah (1459–1474). Man Singh (1550–1614) realized the civil and military leverage of Dhaka and made it a *thana* (military district). Bakht Binat's Mosque, the oldest surviving structure in Dhaka from the pre-Mughal era, was built during the reign of Sultan Nasir al-Din Mahmud Shah I (1433–1459).

Generally, pre-Mughal Dhaka remains neglected as a field of scholarly research. Abdul Karim, preeminent historian of medieval Bengal and author of *Dacca: The Mughal Capital* (1964), encapsulates this view:

"Dhaka, a place of some importance in the Sultanate period, came to the lime-light of history under the Mughals. The Mughals first established a thana (fortified post) at Dhaka to guard the imperial position against the incursions of the independent or semi-independent 'Bhuyia' chiefs. The flotilla of war-boats was also posted near the thana for the same purpose under Admiral Shah Bardi. Dhaka thus started as a thana establishment in the reign of Akbar.

But the city acquired fame and glory only after being capital of the Subah in the reign of Jahangir in 1610 AD."

The standard timeline, from the Mughal period onward, goes something like this. The arrival of Mughal Governor of Bengal Islam Khan Chishti in the early 17th century marks the beginning of the Mughal period, and the city rose to prominence as a provincial Mughal capital. Its growth slowed when Mughal Governor Murshid Quli Khan transferred the capital to Murshidabad in 1703. Dhaka became a pale shadow of its former self during the time of the British East India Company and, subsequently, the British colonial administration in the 18th and 19th centuries. Dhaka again claimed the spotlight, when it became the provincial capital of East Bengal and Assam in 1905, during the inchoate partition of Bengal. After the Indian Partition (1947), it was established as the capital of East Pakistan and, in 1971, as the national capital of the independent nation of Bangladesh.

Dhaka's pre-Partition architectural footprint—namely, Mughal and colonial—is rather modest, compared with such cities as Delhi, Agra, Lahore, Mumbai (formerly Bombay), and Chennai (formerly Madras). This guidebook includes four representative buildings from the pre Partition period. The Pakistan era (1947–1971), particularly the so-called Decade of Development (1958–1968), was a fertile time for architectural development in Dhaka. Five buildings, including Muzharul Islam's Faculty of Fine Arts and Louis Kahn's National Assembly building (also known as the Parliament building), showcase this period's paradigmatic building activities.

Bangladesh emerged as an independent nation in 1971, after a bloody liberation war. As in any other post-independence country, the decade of the 1970s in Bangladesh was a period of nation-building, economic chaos, political turmoil, and intense identity politics. Slowly but steadily, the country dealt with its poverty and tempestuous political conditions. Increased trade, export-oriented manufacturing (particularly the ready-made garment industry), and industrialization bolstered the national economy, although at a great environmental cost. The city's open spaces, water resources, and peripheral arable lands were either built up or filled up and occupied by politically influential land-grabbers.

Despite some setbacks, the public and the private sectors flourished, and many non-governmental organizations (NGOs) played key roles in poverty alleviation and social advancement. With a growing economy and an increasingly assertive middle class, the country's architectural scene became vibrant. Various national design competitions, the rise of an urban middle class and its growing aesthetic consciousness, and the emergence of real estate developers in the early 1990s helped promote architecture as a serious career choice. From the late 1980s onward, architecture emerged as a sociocultural force. Sixteen buildings in this guidebook highlight Dhaka's architectural development during this period.

Although intended as an architectural travel resource, *DAC: Dhaka* interprets buildings within an art-historical framework, based on the premise that architecture is deeply intertwined with multifaceted human conditions. As you explore Dhaka and its architecture, I hope that this guidebook serves as a knowledgeable companion.

Adnan Morshed
Washington, DC
January 2017

ABOUT THE GUIDE

As Dean MacCannell argued in *The Tourist* (1976; rev. ed. 2013), tourism is the most visible and contested expression of modernity. And, this architectural guidebook for Dhaka reflects a new sociology of modern tourism, much different from past generations. Today's world travelers have developed a profound curiosity about people and cultures, cities and architecture, landscape and ecology.

Modern tourists also visit more places than ever before, but don't spend a lot of time in one location. They allow, perhaps, a maximum of three days per city. And, during those three days, they can explore 25 buildings with some intellectual satisfaction.

In Dhaka, a city of 18 million and ever-sprawling, dense urban areas, an inquisitive observer can experience a broad range of exceptional adventures—especially in architecture.

This guidebook focuses on 25 buildings in Dhaka, representing different architectural phases since the Mughal era, beginning in the early 17th century. (The earliest surviving structure in Dhaka is a small pre-Mughal mosque in Old Dhaka.) The list is neither exhaustive, nor necessarily representative of the "best" in town. Rather, the goal is to narrate the stories of the city through the buildings that played transformative roles in its architectural formation. The featured buildings (a) communicate larger ideas about Dhaka's building tradition, (b) represent an architectural trend, (c) influence the architectural scene, and (d) offer a spatial story in the evolution of this city.

As a traveler's resource, this guidebook combines nuanced architectural and urban histories of these buildings, along with maps, drawings, and pictures. It also includes practical information, such as Dhaka's climate; languages; travel, hotel, and restaurant options; currency; and markets and shops, among other helpful details.

The concept for an architectural guidebook for Dhaka dawned on me in 2013, after I had led 40 members of the Society of Architectural Historians on a study tour of three capitals: New Delhi, Chandigarh, and Dhaka. While preparing a reference booklet prior to the trip, I realized that in-depth resource books for architectural travels to the subcontinent were scarce. This lacuna, unfortunately, contributes to a lack of informed travel; hinders efficient itinerary planning; and, sadly, reinforces Orientalist tropes regarding non-Western architecture.

While the number of publications on buildings in non-Western countries is increasing, as part of a growing revisionist awareness of the global history of architecture, there remains little in the way of architectural guidebooks for cities outside the West. This book strives to fill this void. It broadens the scope of architectural knowledge, while bridging building appreciation and tourism, to their mutual benefit.

Adnan Morshed
Washington, DC
January 2017

DHAKA-ARICHA HWY
11
D
R504
22B

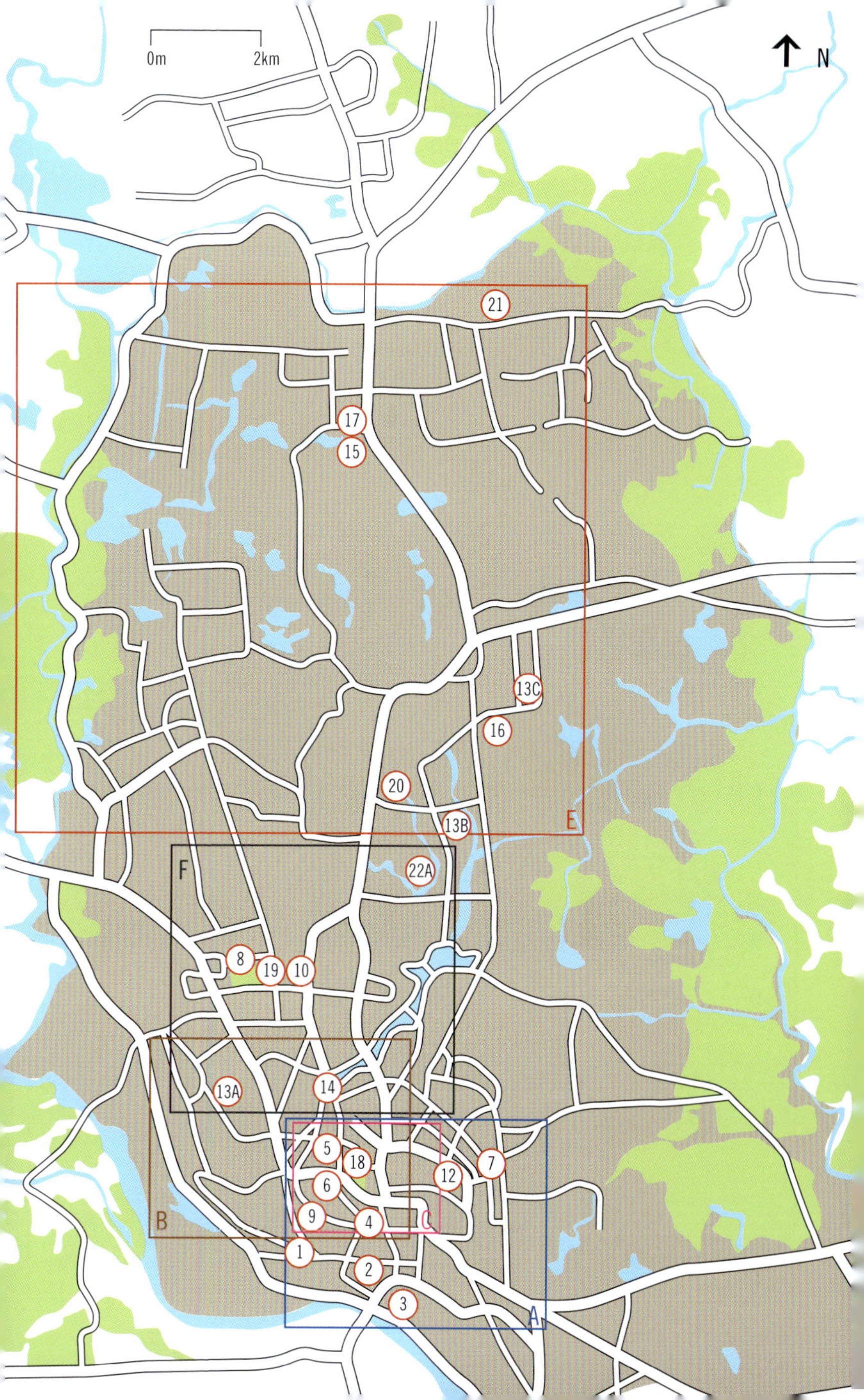

0m
2km
N
A
B
C
E
F
1
2
3
4
5
6
7
8
9
10
12
13A
13B
13C
14
15
16
17
18
19
20
21
22A

0m 500m 1km

ZOOM A

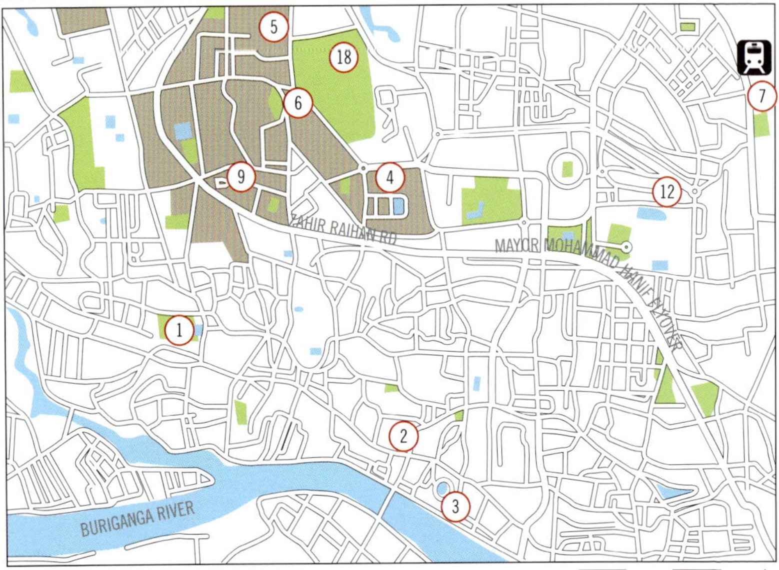

0m 500m 1km

ZOOM B

ZOOM C

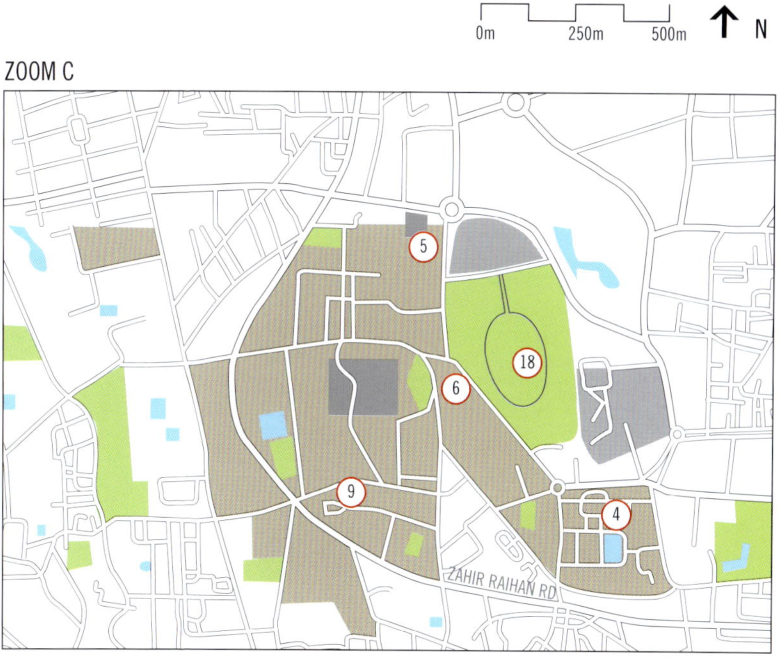

1 Lalbagh Fort Complex
2 Armenian Church of the Holy Resurrection
3 Ahsan Manzil
4 Curzon Hall
5 Faculty of Fine Arts
6 Teacher–Student Center (TSC)
7 Kamalapur Railway Station
9 Department of Architecture Building
12 Bangladesh Chemical Industries Corporation (BCIC) Headquarters
13A Kamaluddin Residence
14 Priyo Prangan Apartment Complex
18 Museum of Independence and Independence Monument

ZOOM D

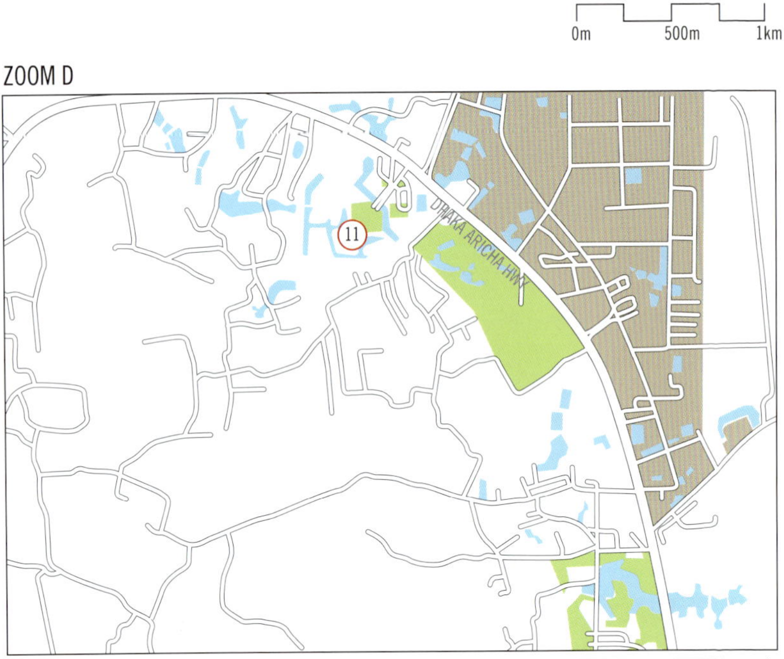

ZOOM E

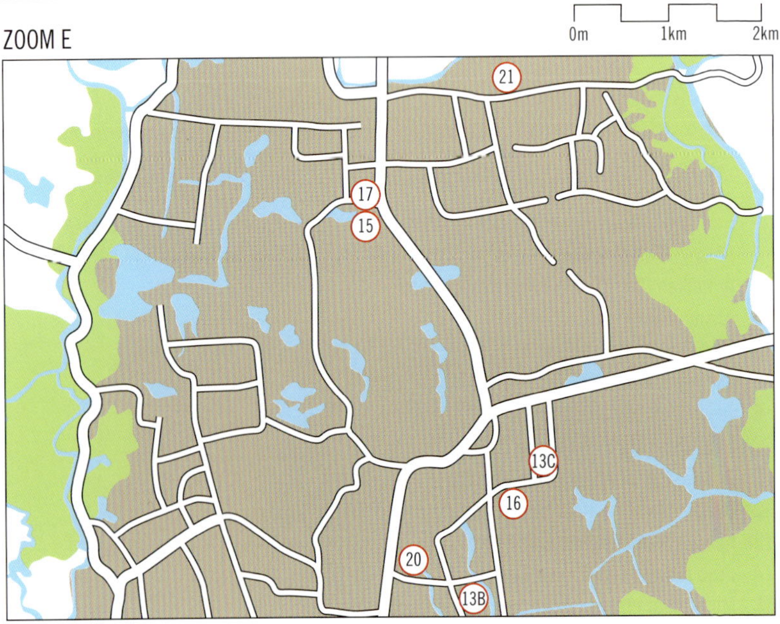

ZOOM F

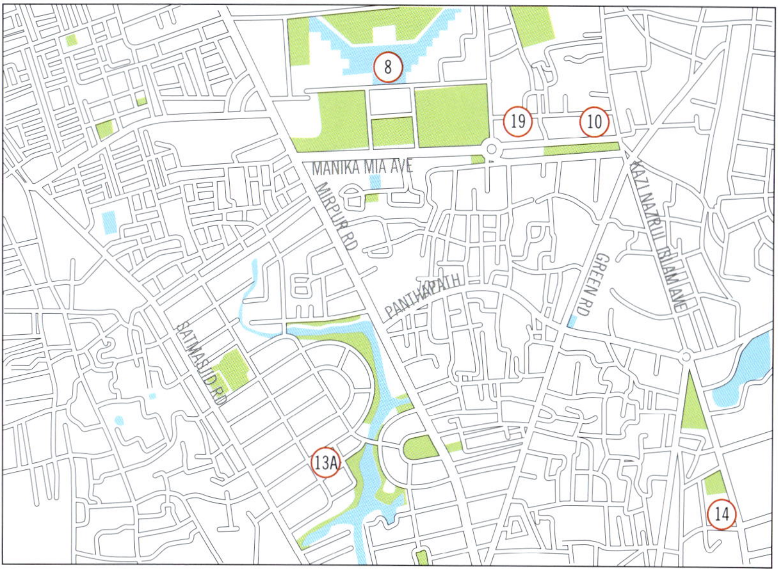

8 National Assembly Building (Jatiyo Shangshad Bhaban)
10 Bangladesh Agricultural Research Council (BARC) Headquarters
11 National Martyrs' Memorial (Jatiyo Smriti Shoudho)
13A Kamaluddin Residence
13B S. A. Residence
13C Karim Residence
14 Priyo Prangan Apartment Complex
15 Scholastica School
16 Grameenphone Corporate Headquarters (GP House)
17 BRAC–Aarong Commercial Center
19 Krishibid Institution of Bangladesh (KIB)
20 Akash Prodip Apartment Building
21 Bait Ur Rouf Mosque

DHAKA
IN 25 BUILDINGS

1 Lalbagh Fort Complex
2 Armenian Church of the Holy Resurrection
3 Ahsan Manzil
4 Curzon Hall
5 Faculty of Fine Arts
6 Teacher–Student Center (TSC)
7 Kamalapur Railway Station
8 National Assembly Building (Jatiyo Shangshad Bhaban)
9 Department of Architecture Building
10 Bangladesh Agricultural Research Council (BARC) Headquarters
11 National Martyrs' Memorial (Jatiyo Smriti Shoudho)
12 Bangladesh Chemical Industries Corporation (BCIC) Headquarters
13A Kamaluddin Residence

13B S. A. Residence
13C Karim Residence
14 Priyo Prangan Apartment Complex
15 Scholastica School
16 Grameenphone Corporate Headquarters (GP House)
17 BRAC–Aarong Commercial Center
18 Museum of Independence and Independence Monument
19 Krishibid Institution of Bangladesh (KIB)
20 Akash Prodip Apartment Building
21 Bait Ur Rouf Mosque
22A JAAGO Foundation School
22B Arcadia Education and Vocational Training Project

1. LALBAGH FORT COMPLEX

LOCATION: Lalbagh, Dhaka 1211
ARCHITECT: Unknown
CONSTRUCTION: 1678–1679

PRACTICAL INFORMATION:

The Lalbagh Fort Complex is open to the public. There is an entry fee. See "Facts for the Visitor," p. 158, for details.

1 Lalbagh Fort Complex
2 Armenian Church of the Holy Resurrection
3 Ahsan Manzil

NEARBY ATTRACTIONS:

A Dhakeshwari Temple
B Buriganga River
C Dhaka Central Jail

Unlike Mughal Emperor Akbar's planned capital at Fatehpur Sikri in Agra or Shah Jahan's capital in Delhi—both constructed with a unitary concept over a relatively short time span—Mughal-era provincial capitals like Dhaka (or Lahore) grew piecemeal, during an extended period of time. Little archaeological and textual evidence exists to suggest that any kind of holistic urban system influenced Mughal Dhaka's growth. Instead, the city's building blocks expanded slowly along the river and northward, by needs-based spatial accretions within localized configurations.

As for the city's architectural growth, Dhaka never received the kind of imperial patronage that was lavished on North Indian capitals like Delhi, Agra, and Lahore. The European travelers visiting Bengal during the Mughal heyday painted a modest picture of Mughal Dhaka. Niccolao Manucci (1639–1717), Venetian writer and traveler, who worked in the Mughal court in various capacities, described Dhaka in his anecdotal *Storia do Mogor*, although the veracity of many of his claims has been questioned. Visiting Dhaka in 1663, the year Shaista Khan had assumed the vice royalty of Bengal, Manucci described Dhaka as "neither strong nor large, but had many inhabitants; most of its houses were made of straw." During his visit to Dhaka in 1666, Jean-Baptiste Tavernier (1605–1689) observed that Dhaka was predominantly characterized by a linear urban morphology along the Buriganga River, as city-dwellers built houses in the hygienic waterfront area.

A better understanding of Mughal Dhaka's urban and architectural footprints requires insights into the Mughal attitude toward the city, located more or less at the geographic heart of the Bengal delta. This attitude influenced the ways that Mughal Dhaka began. As eminent historian of medieval Bengal Abdul Karim (1928–2007) described, Dhaka developed from a modest settlement to a provincial Mughal capital in 1608 or 1610 (the exact year remains contested) and enjoyed the capital status under the Mughals for the next 100 years. The decision to shift the capital of Bengal from Rajmahal (in northeastern India and on the western bank of the Ganges) to Dhaka is generally credited to Islam Khan Chishti, the Mughal Subahdar or Governor of Bengal, who was a member of the Fatehpur Sikri Sufi family and a

grandson of Emperor Akbar's chief spiritual guide, Shaikh Salim Chishti. Located on the northern bank of the Buriganga River, Dhaka's connectivity to surrounding districts through waterways convinced the Mughal bureaucracy to envision the city as an outpost at the empire's southeastern frontier.

Two key factors contributed to Dhaka's growth during the Mughal era. First, the city's superior geo-strategic location enabled both the surveillance of lower Bengal, which had been ravaged by the Maghs and Portuguese pirates, and the suppression of rebel chiefs. And, second, Dhaka's geography also provided an administrative advantage in collecting imperial revenues and protecting revenue interests. According to Karim, "No official estimate of the population during the Mughal period exists today." However, when Portuguese monk Sebastian Manrique traveled to Dhaka in 1640, he estimated that the population of an expanded Dhaka was about 200,000.

Yet, despite Dhaka's military and commercial advantages, the Delhi-Agra-based Mughal emperors considered ruling Bengal a challenging undertaking, an issue related to their perception of Bengal. In addition to the long distance from North India, Bengal's humid climate—combined with its unique geography, crisscrossed by countless rivulets; its marshy swamps; and its prolonged monsoon season—allegedly gave rise to an ambivalent Mughal attitude toward the Bengal delta as a land of insurmountable remoteness. In the Mughal imagination, Bengal, also called Bhati, was some kind of "Wild East," away from the seat of imperial power. The Mughal view of Dhaka as both a useful frontier outpost and a distant and climatically challenged place perhaps explains why the city does not have a robust Mughal architectural footprint. There are no Taj Mahals, grand mosques, or Shalimar Gardens.

Thus, visitors interested in Dhaka's Mughal architecture will gain a historically nuanced understanding only if they learn how the Mughal powerbase in North India conceptually framed Bengal.

Despite Dhaka's modest Mughal heritage, visitors would be surprised to see a dynamic range of the empire's contribution to the city: mosques, mausoleums, minarets and *i'dgahs*, forts and *katras*,

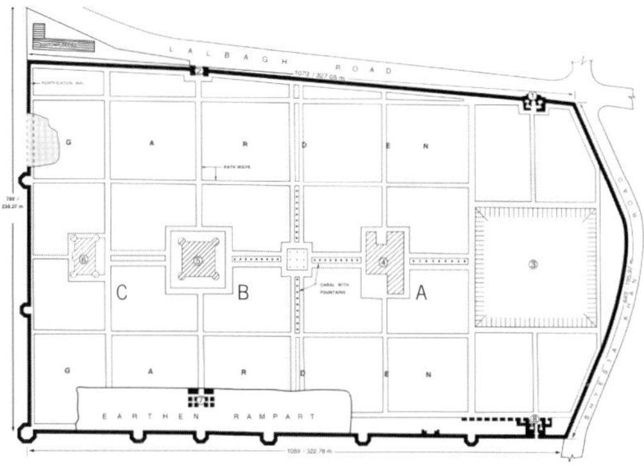

A Audience Hall (Diwan-i-Khas) and Bathing Chamber (Hammam)
B Tomb of Bibi Pari (Mausoleum)
C Mosque

Lalbagh Fort Complex: site plan

palaces and *hammams* (bathing chambers), *Qadam rasuls* and Imambaras, and bridges. The key Mughal elements that were introduced to the local architectural scene were dominant central domes, lofty axial entrances set in a central projecting bay (for emphasis), and an axial plan. The Mughals replaced Bengal's traditional terra-cotta art with plaster panels. Canonical historiographies of the deltaic region's architecture focus on how Mughal edifices in Bengal were based mostly on the Mughal art and architectural traditions that had developed in North India. However, what has not been researched adequately is the other direction of aesthetic influence. Nazimuddin Ahmed stated that "such unmistakable Bengali elements as the curved eaves and ridge" were diffused "to such places as Lahore, Delhi, Agra, and even as far as distant Rajputana."

The Mughal structures that are located in and around Dhaka might be modest in scale, architectural scope, or artistic excellence, but they offer great insights into the cultural politics of the Mughal Empire's southeastern frontier.

Lalbagh Fort

"Standing within Lalbagh one readily recalls the great palace-garden complexes at Lahore, Delhi, and Agra and realizes that this could only have been conceived and built by outsiders to Bengal. No element of the complex is indigenous to the delta."—Richard Eaton, 1996

The best example of Mughal building art in Dhaka is the incomplete palace complex of Lalbagh Fort. Undertaken 25 years after the Taj Mahal was built, Lalbagh Fort is constructed on approximately 7 ha (18 acres) of land in the southwestern part of Old Dhaka. The fort was originally called Killa Aurangabad (Aurangabad Fort), named after the Mughal Emperor Aurangajeb by his third son and the fort's patron Prince Muhammad Azam (1653–1707). British Collector of Dhaka Charles D'Oyly's sketch titled *Bastion of the Lal Bagh, Dacca* (made between 1808 and 1817) offers an impression that the fort once stood on the bank of the Buriganga River, which has now shifted to the south. The name Lalbagh suggests that it was once a garden of Mughal origin, as in Mughal parlance *bāgh* or *bagicha* means garden.

Historian Ahmad Hasan Dani (1920–2009) mentioned that "the name Lalbagh is difficult to explain, except on assumption that there was a garden on this spot before the fort came into existence." Today, the fort complex, surrounded by a 6.1 m (20 ft.) high defensive wall with semi-octagonal bastions, feels like an oasis in the midst of a bustling old city—its narrow, winding streets filled with shops, vendors, pedestrians, and vehicles of all types. The Archaeology Department of the Government of Bangladesh restored Lalbagh Fort, and it is a major tourist attraction.

Prince Azam initiated the construction of Lalbagh Fort in 1678, during his 15-month-long vice royalty of Bengal, but abandoned the project when Emperor Aurangajeb summoned him to Delhi. His successor, Shaista Khan, continued the construction work. However, in 1684, Khan's daughter Iran-Dukht, also known as Bibi Pari, died unexpectedly. He suspended work on the complex, believing that her death was an omen. Some observers think that the purpose of the fort was to provide safe accommodation to Subahdars during their stay in Bengal. To some, it is a miniature version of the grand palace fortresses built by the Mughals in their capitals in North India.

Upon entry, the visitor finds an axial, symmetrical, and geometrical layout of a lush green garden. The oblong site, measuring approximately 329.8 m by 213.4 m (1,082 ft. by 700 ft.) along the east-west axis, includes three grand gateways: two in the north and one in the south. The southern gateway is the most monumental. Rising three stories, its main entrance consists of a stone-framed archway set within a half-dome, flanked by octagonal turrets. The domed entrance chamber comprises guardrooms on either side.

Once inside, the visitor finds three main edifices that interrupt the expansive garden grid: from east to west, Diwan-i-Khas (the Audience Hall) and the Hammam (Bathing Chamber); Bibi Pari's tomb; and the three-domed mosque. All of these structures are on the central axis and are inscribed by a water channel that is equipped with fountains. A large pond is also on this axis, the east of the Audience Hall. Recent archaeology has unearthed remains of more than 25 structures, including those for water supply and

sewerage, roof gardens, a water reservoir, and fountains. Together, they reveal the advanced hydrological engineering system that serviced the fort complex.

To protect Lalbagh Fort from riverside attack, it was surrounded by two high brick walls on the south. The outer wall is about 6.1 m (20 ft.) high and 1.37 m (4.5 ft.) thick, while the inner one is 13.7 m (45 ft.) high with the same thickness.

In 1717, when Murshid Quli Khan, Subahdar of Bengal, shifted the capital of Bengal from Dhaka to Murshidabad, Dhaka lost its glory, and so did Lalbagh Fort. The British took lease of the fort in 1844 and converted it into a police headquarters. During the colonial era, the British undertook extensive construction activities inside Lalbagh Fort—including additions and alterations to existing edifices—without any regard to the original design. The Department of Archaeology has removed all of the buildings constructed by the British administration.

Audience Hall (Diwan-i-Khas) and Bathing Chamber (Hammam)

The Audience Hall is a two-story multipurpose structure that serves as the Mughal Governor's residence, a meeting hall or the Audience Hall, and the Bathing Chamber (Hammam). The Audience Hall, measuring 8.1 m by 5.6 m (26 ft. 7 in. by 18 ft. 3 in.) and containing a sunken ornamental fountain, is approached by a three-bay arched entrance on the east. It is flanked by two square chambers along the north-south axis, containing staircases that lead to the upper floor. The ground floor plan is repeated on the upper floor to accommodate residential quarters. On the exterior, the ground floor wall presents an elaborate system of recessed niches, and the upper floor has arched windows covered by *jali* (stone screens).

An imposing arched doorway on the interior western wall of the Audience Hall leads to the central Bathing Chamber through a half-dome. The chamber's original domical roof had an opening admitting light and allowing ventilation. Colorful glazed tiles embellish the floor. This chamber demonstrates an elaborate system of hydraulic engineering, recalling

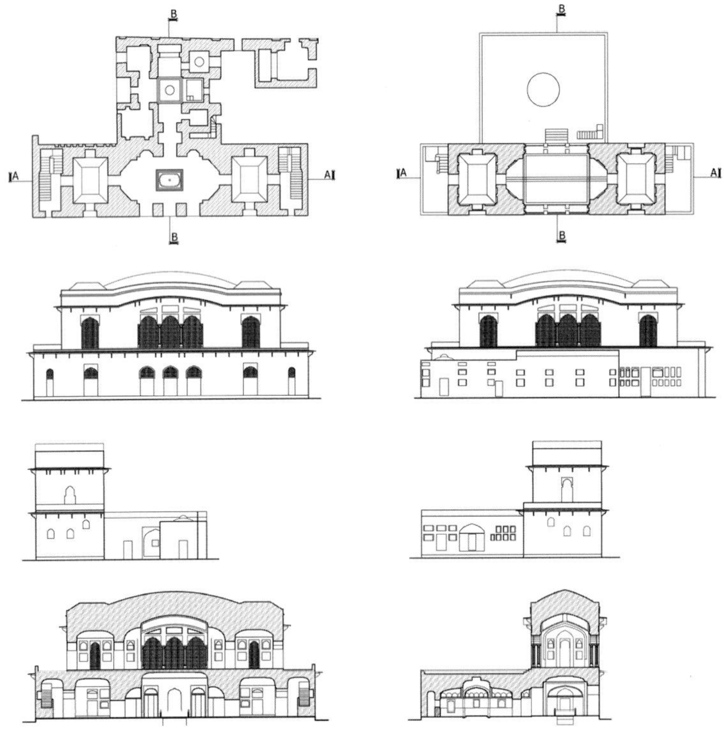

Audience Hall and Bathing Chamber: plans, elevations, and sections

the history of Roman baths. To the north, steps lead to a masonry tank, which probably contained temperate waters for bathing. A series of adjacent rooms housed a system for heating water, a private chamber, and a toilet with dressing room—all equipped with covered drains. There was also provision for discharging wastewater into a large masonry vaulted drain, west of the entire complex.

The Audience Hall is a striking case of hybrid architecture. The curvilinear *do-chala* (two sloping sides) roof over the central hall is reminiscent of the archetypal Bengal hut's gabled roof and drooping eaves, an architectural synthesis that had already appeared in Mughal buildings in the north, such as Red Fort, in Delhi, and Fatehpur Sikri, in Agra.

Tomb of Bibi Pari (Mausoleum)
Bibi Pari's tomb is based on the characteristic Mughal square plan for mausoleums, featuring a central domed chamber. Examples include the Humayun's tomb (1570) in Delhi and the Taj Mahal (1653) in Agra. With 20.1 m (66 ft.) long symmetrical sides, the tomb is located on a raised platform at the center of a square garden, as in earlier Mughal edifices. A false central dome, sheathed in copper and topped by a finial, crowns the building. Four octagonal turrets, capped by plastered kiosks with ribbed cupolas, hold the building mass of the tomb. The siting of the impressive building reflects the established tradition of the Mughal *charbagh* (four gardens) planning principle.

The symmetrical interior is divided into nine chambers, including the central chamber, which measures 5.8 m (19 ft.) on each side. Veneered in white marble, this chamber includes a stepped cenotaph at the center, embellished with floral motifs in relief and marked as a female grave by a *takhti* motif on top. The interior walls of the tomb chamber and the ceilings of the other eight rooms are clad in imported white marble and black basalt, respectively. Bibi Pari's tomb is the most impressive building among the surviving structures of Lalbagh Fort.

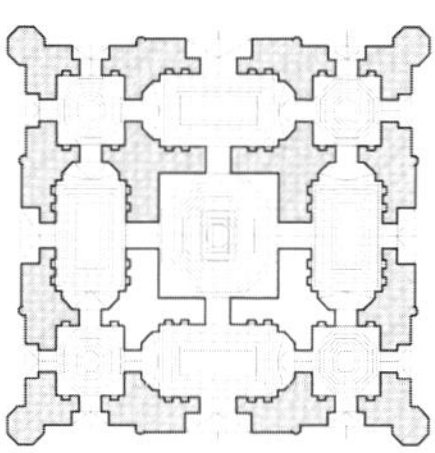

Ground floor plan

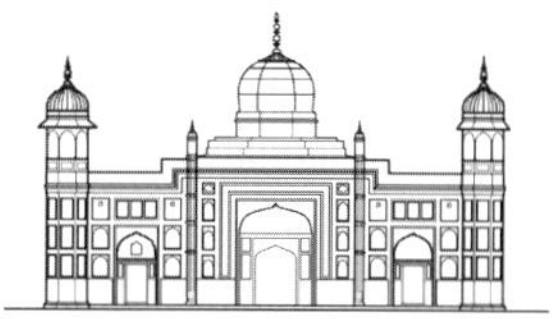

Front elevation

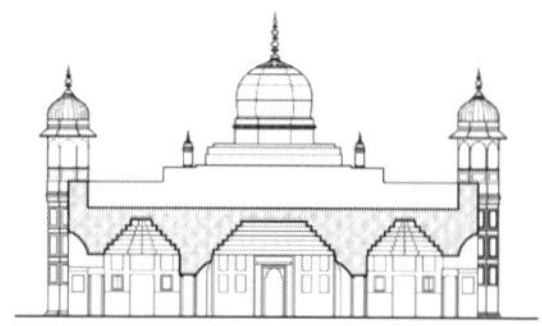

Section

Lalbagh Fort Mosque

A provincial version of North Indian three-domed Mughal Jami mosques (the main congregational mosque of the town), Lalbagh Fort's mosque is oblong in plan, measuring 19.8 m by 9.8 m (65 ft. by 32 ft.). This model became known locally as the Shaista Khan Style, as it was most likely built during the reign of Shaista Khan.

The three-domed mosque was first noticed in India during the Lodi (1451–1526) and Suri (1540–1556) periods. This design continued under the patronage of the Imperial Mughals, as exemplified by the famous Jami mosques in Delhi, Agra, and Fatehpur Sikri, all of which feature three-domed prayer halls. Later, this style was introduced to Bengal and modified by local craftsmen.

The plan of Lalbagh Fort mosque is divided into three bays. Two lateral arches define the larger central bay, which is square, while the side ones are rectangular. All three domes rise above the bays and are carried on squinches or pendentives (the curved triangular plane that supports a dome over a square base). The central four-centered dome is larger and higher than the two side bulbous domes (a pointed dome that swells). All of the domes are fluted and raised on octagonal drums. Four octagonal turrets or minarets at the four corners of the structure rise slightly above the parapet. The east elevation consists of three high multicusped arches. Façades are decorated with recessed rectangular panels.

Some scholars argue that the side domes might have been reconstructed in the late 18th century because the bulbous dome is unprecedented in Bengal before this date.

Front elevation

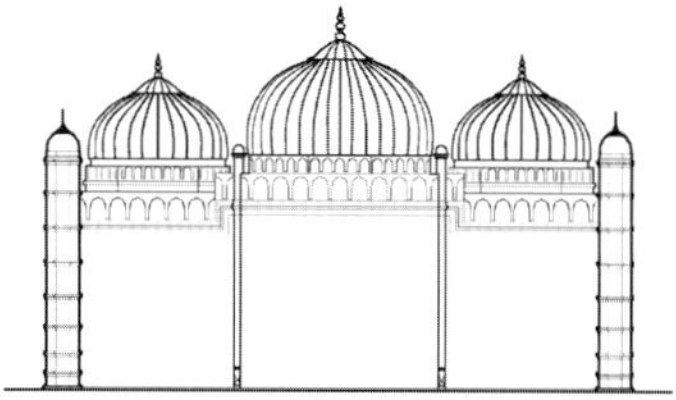

Back elevation

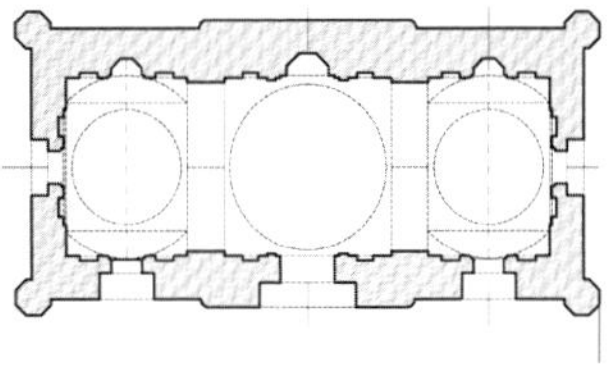

Plan

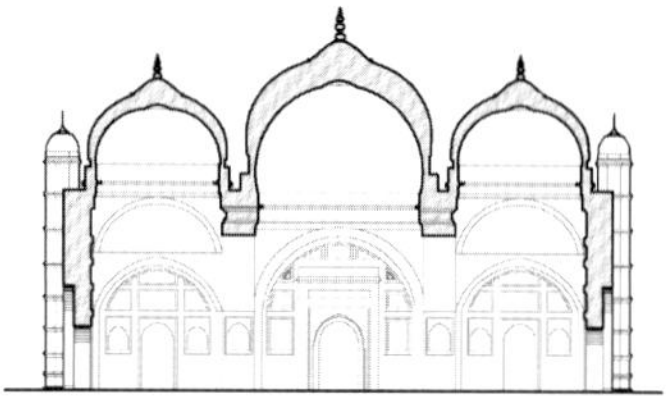

Section

Side elevation

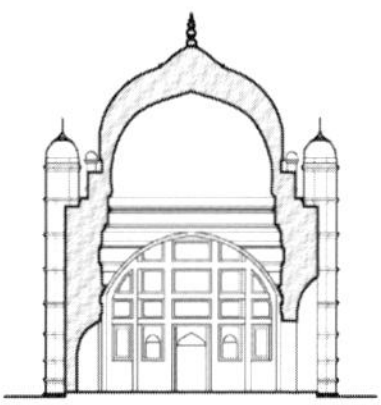

Section

Section

2. ARMENIAN CHURCH OF THE HOLY RESURRECTION

LOCATION: Armanitola Road, Nayabazar, Dhaka 1100
ARCHITECT: Unknown
CONSTRUCTION: 1781

PRACTICAL INFORMATION:

The Armenian Church of the Holy Resurrection is open only to those with foreign passports.

1 Lalbagh Fort Complex
2 Armenian Church of the Holy Resurrection
3 Ahsan Manzil

NEARBY ATTRACTIONS:

A Buriganga River
B Badamtoli Boat Terminal

The Armenian Church of the Holy Resurrection on Armanitola Road in Old Dhaka is modest in its architectural scope, yet its history presents a rich tapestry of the Armenian footprint on the commerce, politics, and education of East Bengal. More important, the church is an architectural testament to the story of how the Armenian diasporas spread out from their historic homeland, located between the Black Sea and the Caspian Sea, to far-flung regions and thrived as a versatile cosmopolitan community.

Armenia occupies a crucial geographic location at the intersection of various civilizations and trading routes, such as the Silk Road from China to Rome. A vital link between East and West, the country was under the domination of various competing political powers, including the Persians, the Greeks, the Romans, the Arabs, the Persians again, the Ottomans, and the Russians. Their long political subjugation, on the one hand, made it difficult for them to maintain their Christian faith, language, culture, and national identity. (The Armenians were the first people to embrace Christianity as a state religion in 301 CE.) On the other hand, challenging circumstances exhorted Armenians to be resilient in the face of political repression, to develop entrepreneurial acumen and mediating skills, and to be a "trade diaspora."

There is no consensus on exactly when the Armenians arrived in Dhaka. Some historians, however, suggest that they were in Bengal in the early 17th century, most likely arriving with the southbound migration of Armenian diasporas from Persia. Because the official language of the Mughal court was Persian, the Persian-speaking Armenians could easily adapt to life in the Mughal Empire. Being skillful in the textile business, the Armenians naturally gravitated to Dhaka, one of the trading hubs for fine textiles, contributing significantly to the city's commercial life. In addition to textiles and raw silk, the Armenians also engaged in the trade of saltpeter (used as gunpowder), salt, and betel nut. They pioneered jute trading in the second half of the 19th century and popularized tea drinking in Bengal. When they began to lose the textile business to the British private traders in the late 18th century, the Armenians reoriented their focus to landholding, eventually becoming prominent and wealthy *zamindars* (landowners). Examples of Armenian zamindars in Dhaka

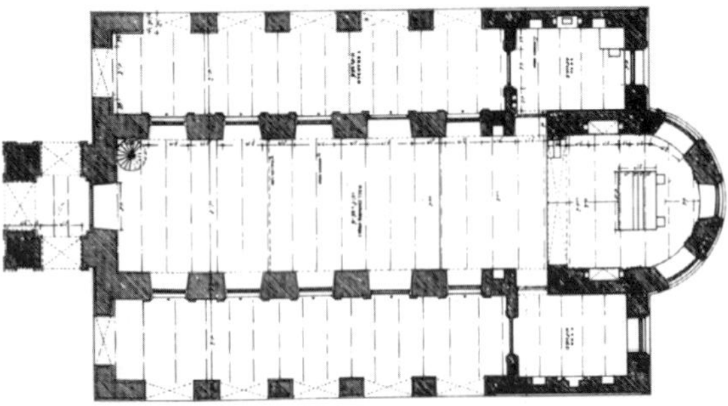

Plan

include Agha Aratoon Michael, Agha Sarkies, and Nicholas Marcar Pogose.

Compared with those in Calcutta and Madras, Dhaka's well-knit Armenian community was small but wealthy, exerting a great deal of influence on local and regional businesses. The Armenians resided in Armanitola, an Old Dhaka neighborhood (*mahalla*) that was named after the colony where they once lived (although not all Armenians lived there). Many of Dhaka's wealthy Armenians lived in European-style bungalows in Old Dhaka. One of the most famous was the Ruplal House (now derelict), built by the Armenian zamindar Aratoon.

The religious life of the community revolved around the Armenian Church of the Holy Resurrection, built in 1781 on the ruins of an earlier chapel and cemetery. It is worthwhile to note that the Armenians built their first churches in Madras (now Chennai), in 1547; in Agra, in 1562; and in Calcutta, in 1724. The Portuguese built

Section

the first church in Dhaka in 1679 and reconstructed it in 1769, a decade or so before the Armenians built their church in Old Dhaka.

The land for the Armenian Church was originally gifted by the Armenian nobleman Agha Catchick Minas, whose wife died in 1764; she is buried inside the church. The church galvanized the community around the Sunday mass and other religious festivals. In 1840, Lt. Colonel Davidson of British Bengal Engineers provided a vivid portrayal of the Christmas celebration at this church.

The Armenian Church stands today like a quiet and dignified monument amidst the frenzied urban growth surrounding it. Residential apartment towers dwarf its two-story structure and the belfry (or the bell tower). The oblong plan of the church is a simple basilica type with a double-height nave flanked by a pair of one-story, 4.27 m (14 ft.) wide arcades that open to the surrounding graveyard. The three-tier

Nave, looking toward altar

bell tower, capped with a conical roof, on the west provides a square-shaped and arched vestibule, followed by a ceremonial entrance to the nave.

Running along the east-west axis, the nave space is boldly articulated by five heavy piers on either side. The piers are spanned by both doors and windows. Rows of wooden pews flank the central processional aisle of the nave, creating a linear progression of space toward a semicircular apse. The eastern end of the nave is visually framed by a tall arch, behind which is the projecting apse containing an elevated altar. A 3.05 m (10 ft.) wooden altarpiece contains an artistic depiction of *The Last Supper*. Two identical sanctuaries, accessible from the nave, flank the apse. Located above the roof line of the aisles, skylights along the nave walls bring light deep inside the church. As one enters the nave space, to the left is a circular wooden staircase that ascends to the second floor gallery, overlooking the nave, and then to the third floor of the belfry.

Although the style of the church seems somewhat eclectic at first, a closer inspection reveals that its typology is based on typical features of Armenian church architecture. The bell tower's ribbed conical steeple, surmounted with a cross, is common to well-known examples of Armenian churches. These include the Cathedral of Holy Etchmiadzin near Yerevan in Armenia (originally built in the 4th century and rebuilt in its present form in the 17th century; this is considered the oldest church in the world); St. Hripsime in Etchmiadzin, Armenia (rebuilt in 618 CE); the Armenian Church on Lake Van in the East Anatolia Province, Turkey (10th century); and the Armenian Church of the Holy Nazareth (1724) near the Howrah Bridge in Kolkata. All of these churches have the paradigmatic "drum-and-cone pattern" that inspired Dhaka's Armenian Church. The arched base of its bell tower acts as a pronaos for the church proper and is common to all of the examples mentioned above, except the one in East Anatolia. The circular windows facing cardinal directions that we find on the steeple of the Dhaka church are strikingly similar to those of the Armenian Church in Kolkata. An interesting feature of the church in Old Dhaka is how its belfry is balanced out on the east, where the balustrade on the nave roof culminates in a Baroque crown-like

Graveyard

detail, with a cross on top and an elliptical opening at the center.

The high boundary wall around the Armenian Church in Dhaka shields the property from rampant land speculation. The main entrance to the site is from the east, near the circular apse. Visitors must walk through the graveyard all the way to the western forecourt of the church. Reading the tombstones of the graveyard feels like a journey back to a time when the Armenians played pivotal roles in the life of the city. The church, along with its somber graveyard, in the midst of noisy city life, seems like a dignified and somewhat melancholic symbol of a distant past.

3. AHSAN MANZIL

LOCATION: Nawab Ahsanullah Road (near Sadarghat-Gabtoli Road), Dhaka 1100
ARCHITECT: Unknown
MASTER PLAN: Martin and Company, UK
CONSTRUCTION: 1859–1872
HISTORIC PRESERVATION: 1985–1989
INAUGUARTED AS A MUSEUM: 1992
AWARD: Architect's Regional Council of Asia Gold Medal, 1992

PRACTICAL INFORMATION:

Ahsan Manzil is open to the public. There is an entry fee. See "Facts for the Visitor," p. 158, for details.

1 Lalbagh Fort Complex
2 Armenian Church of the Holy Resurrection
3 Ahsan Manzil
4 Curzon Hall
9 Department of Architecture Building

NEARBY ATTRACTIONS:

A Gol Talab (water tank)
B Buriganga River
C Badamtoli Boat Terminal

To visit Ahsan Manzil is to learn the colonial-era history of Dhaka. The premises of this palace, (2.23 ha or 5.5 acres), remain today as an architectural reminder of the elite life of the Nawabs of Dhaka during the heyday of the British Raj in the 19th and early 20th centuries. Nawab Khwaja Abdul Ghani (1813–1896), the patriarch of the Nawab family, built the family's official residence and zamindar office—Ahsan Manzil—in 1872 on the bank of the Buriganga River in the Kumartuli area of Old Dhaka. He named the palace after his son, Nawab Khwaja Ahsanullah (1846–1901).

Ahsan Manzil is ostentatiously European in its architectural expression, even though the building's recessed verandahs may recall the Mughal treatment of buildings in a tropical climate. Its triple-arched portal, temple façade capped by a pediment, Greco-Roman column capitals, pilasters, and arched windows—all suggest that it is mostly a European-style building, meshed with some decorative Indian motifs.

Why did the Nawab embrace a European architectural style for his palace? Prior to the advent of British colonial rule, local elites emulated Mughal architecture as their preferred building style, particularly for religious buildings. Charles D'Oyly, the Collector of Dhaka, documented Mughal influence on local buildings with much romance in his book, *Antiquities of Dacca*, published in London around 1820. However, with increasing British colonial footprints in India, building design began to reflect the influence of European styles from the last quarter of the 18th century. Many zamindars began to construct their bungalows in flamboyant European architectural styles to showcase their status, wealth, and power.

In *Buildings of the British Raj in Bangladesh* (1986), Nazimuddin Ahmed wrote: "During the 18th and 19th centuries, the chief interests of the aristocratic feudal lords of the land—familiarly known as zamindars, who often held courtesy titles of 'Rajas' and 'Maharajas'—were not only in European dress, wine, horses, and external glamours of life, but also in architectural forms and embellishments avidly emulating the West for their pretentious country houses or palaces. Often these picturesque palaces combined European Renaissance elements with the fading Mughal architectural forms." Nawab Abdul Ghani's Ahsan Manzil is one such example.

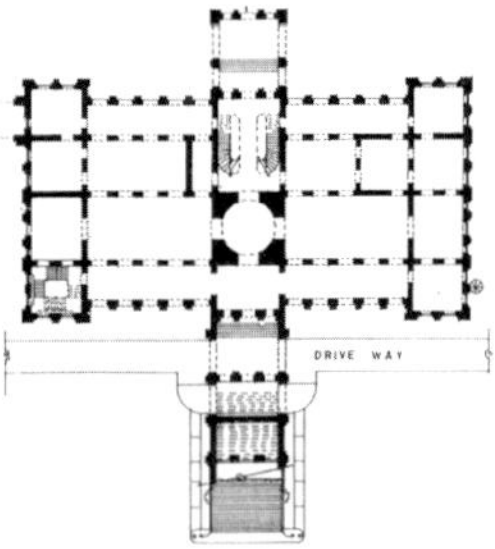

Ground floor plan

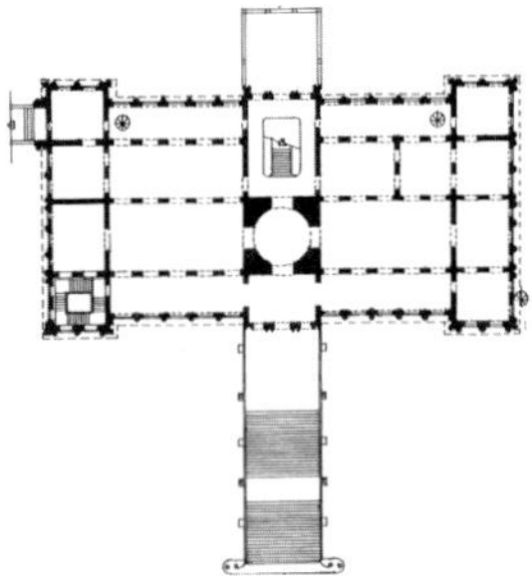

1st floor plan

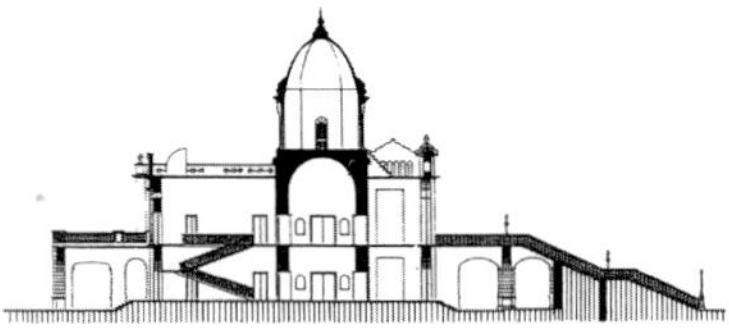

Section

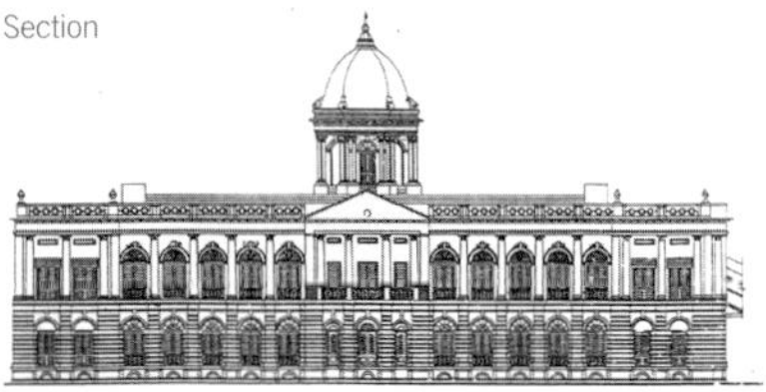

North elevation

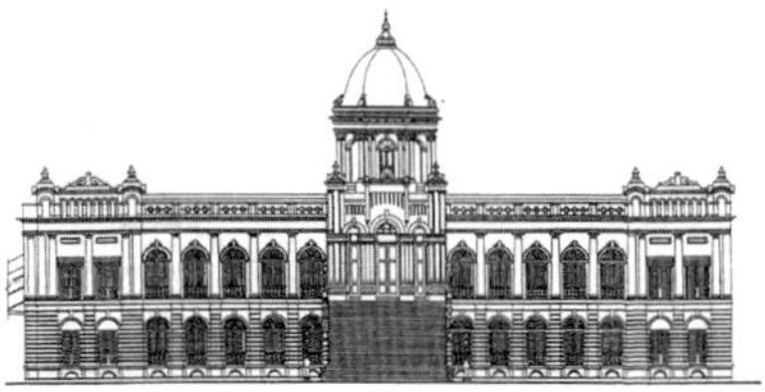

South elevation

Today within the hyper-congested urban growth of Old Dhaka, it is difficult to imagine how this majestic edifice once dominated the riverfront skyline of Dhaka. Colonial-era dignitaries arrived here by luxury boats and ascended its grand flight of stairs, which led to a colorful vestibule and a domed rotunda on the second floor. Lord George Nathaniel Curzon, who took over as Viceroy or Governor General of British India in 1899, came to Dhaka to solicit support for the proposed Partition of Bengal and stayed here as a guest of Nawab Salimullah Bahadur in 1904. Two years later, another momentous event took place in this palace that had crucial political implications for all of India.

Invited by Nawab Salimullah, Muslim leaders from all over the subcontinent congregated at the Durbar Hall of Ahsan Manzil for the 20th Session of the All India Mohammedan Educational Conference in Dhaka, from December 27 to December 29, 1906. Here, on December 30, the

Ahsan Manzil: façade detail

Ahsan Manzil: scale entrance

All India Muslim League was formed, the party that later spearheaded the creation of Pakistan.

Who were the Nawabs of Dhaka? The Khwajas, the forefathers of the Nawabs, migrated to East Bengal—first to Sylhet, then to Dhaka—from Kashmir during the 1730s. When Mughal administration of Dhaka ended in 1843 with the death of Gaziuddin Haider, the last Naib Nazim (Mughal administrator) of the city, the Khwajas took over as the city's "guardians." They occupied such important positions as Commissioner of Dhaka Municipality. In 1867, Abdul Ghani became a member of the Viceroy's Council. As Syed Muhammed Taifoor chronicled in *Glimpses of Old Dhaka* (1956), the Nawab family played crucial roles in the modernization of the city, particularly in the development of educational systems, health care, and urban infrastructure, including the filtered water supply system that served the city population.

Nawab Abdul Ghani emerged not only as a dynamic leader of his clan, but also as the most influential zamindar in the entire East Bengal region in the second half of the 19th century. Nawab Ahsanullah judiciously followed in the footsteps of his illustrious father. Known to be a philanthropist, administrator, generous zamindar, and a learned litterateur, he was appointed to a number of important councils of the colonial administration. He is also credited with the creation of an engineering college, which later became the Bangladesh University of Engineering and Technology, the country's flagship engineering university.

During the Mughal period, according to some historians, zamindar Sheikh Enayetullah of Jamalpur district had a *rongmahal* (pleasure palace) on the present Ahsan Manzil site. Later, French traders bought the palace from Enayetullah's son Motiullah, converting it into a trading outpost and factory. Khwaja Alimullah, the father of Nawab Abdul Ghani, purchased the palace from French traders in 1830 and upgraded the edifice as his family's official residence.

Because his eldest son was deeply pious and uninterested in business and worldly affairs, Khwaja Alimullah made his second son from his second wife, Khwaja Abdul Ghani, the *mutawalli* (manager) of the family estate in 1846. A decade or so later, Abdul Ghani hired Martin and Company, a British construction and engineering firm,

to create a master plan for the site, with Ahsan Manzil as its centerpiece. Construction began in 1859 and ended in 1872. The old building bought from the French traders was converted into *andarmahal* (ladies quarters). The new building became known as Rongmahal and was later renamed Ahsan Manzil.

To this day, Ahsan Manzil remains one of the finest examples of Indo-European architecture in Bangladesh. The two-story building rests on a 1.2 m (4 ft.) high plinth and is crowned with an octagonal dome that soars to 27.1 m (89 ft.) from the ground. With two symmetrical wings on either side of the dome, the building spans a width of 55.8 m (183 ft.). The floor-to-ceiling height is approximately 5.2 m (17 ft.) on the first floor and 5.8 m (19 ft.) on the second floor. The interior space consists of four bays along the east-west axis and five bays along the north-south axis. On the second floor, Darbar Hall and Dance Hall (Jolsha Ghar and Nach Ghar) flank the rotunda on the east and west, respectively. These rooms feature beautifully crafted wooden, vaulted ceilings.

Behind them are two large rooms (*mehman khana*) for entertaining guests. There is a spacious dining room on the first floor, directly below Darbar Hall. The floors of both the dining hall and Darbar Hall are decorated with white, green, and yellow Chinese tiles. Behind the rotunda is a monumental wooden staircase whose wrought iron railings feature vine-leaf motifs. The

walls of the palace are 0.76 m (2.5 ft.) thick. The arched doorways are inlaid with colored glass and stone.

As the influence and prestige of the Nawab family declined in the 20th century and the descendants of the Nawabs became too impoverished to look after such a vast property, the government acquired the Ahsan Manzil premises in 1952, under the East Bengal Estate Acquisition Act. However, many poor descendants of the Nawab family, as well as needy local people, continued to occupy and squat in the palace until the 1970s. They inflicted much damage to the building by indiscriminately altering its configuration. The palace compound degenerated into a slum! Government intervention seemed inevitable.

Realizing the historic and architectural significance of the building, the Government of Bangladesh acquired the property through a Gazette Notification in 1985 and decided to convert it into a national museum. Under the supervision of the Directorate of Public Works and Architecture, the historic preservation of Ahsan Manzil and its premises was completed in 1989. And, Ahsan Manzil opened its doors as a museum in 1992. That same year, Architect's Regional Council of Asia (ARCASIA) honored the restoration project with a Gold Medal. Today, Ahsan Manzil is a popular museum and a major tourist attraction in Old Dhaka.

4. CURZON HALL

LOCATION: University of Dhaka, High Court Street, Dhaka 1000
ARCHITECT: Unknown
CONSTRUCTION: 1904–1908

PRACTICAL INFORMATION:

Visitors to Curzon Hall can see the building from the outside. Permission is required to enter the building.

Contact:
Office of the Registrar
Administrative Building (2nd Floor)
University of Dhaka, Dhaka 1000

Phone: +88-02-9670531/4020
E-Mail: registrar@du.ac.bd

1 Lalbagh Fort Complex
4 Curzon Hall
5 Faculty of Fine Arts
6 Teacher–Student Center (TSC)
9 Department of Architecture Building
18 Museum of Independence and Independence Monument

NEARBY ATTRACTIONS:

A Shaheed Minar (Martyrs' Monument)
B Supreme Court of Bangladesh
C National Eidgah
D Shrine of Three National Leaders
E Tomb and Mosque of Haji Khawja Shahbaz

On October 16, 1905, Dhaka became the capital of the newly created province of East Bengal and Assam, in the wake of what is known as the Partition of Bengal (1905–1911). Although the partition's stated aim was administrative efficiency on the part of the colonial rulers, Viceroy of British India George Nathaniel Curzon (1899–1905) sought to achieve political goals by dividing Bengal. He had hoped that the political autonomy of the Muslims of East Bengal would counterbalance the growing power of the Hindus of West Bengal. Many Hindus viewed the partition as a classic colonial policy of "divide and rule." Muslims of East Bengal, on the other hand, welcomed it as a new opportunity for the development of their region. They long held the grievance that Hindu-dominated West Bengal and its hub Calcutta (now Kolkata) grew as a vast metropolis of trade, education, and Anglo-Indian bourgeois middle-class life, mostly at the expense of East Bengal.

An activist of Muslim regeneration, Nawab Syed Shamsul Huda wrote of this prevailing view among the Muslims: "Before the partition, the largest amount of money used to be spent in districts near Calcutta. The best of colleges, hospitals, and other institutions were founded in or near the capital of India....We have inherited a heritage of the accumulated neglect of years." Dhaka's Nawab Salimullah wrote in an article titled "The New Province—Its Future Possibilities," published in the *Journal of the Moslem Institute*, in 1906: "No one can deny that the partition has roused the entire Mahomedan community of Eastern Bengal. Many poor Mahomedan youths, who had graduated with honours, but were roaming about in search of suitable employment, are now getting prize posts, which they so highly deserved."

One of the most visible transformations of Dhaka as a result of its new status as the capital of East Bengal was in the realm of civic architecture and urban infrastructure. To prepare the provincial capital, the colonial administration acquired sprawling land in the verdant Ramna area beyond Dhaka's northern periphery, demarcated by the then-existing railway line. The architectural and urban growth of Ramna helped mitigate Dhaka's backwater reputation, as encapsulated in a report of *The Times* of London, in 1909: "For many years Dacca has been looked on as the back of the beyond, a place devoid of any

Curzon Hall

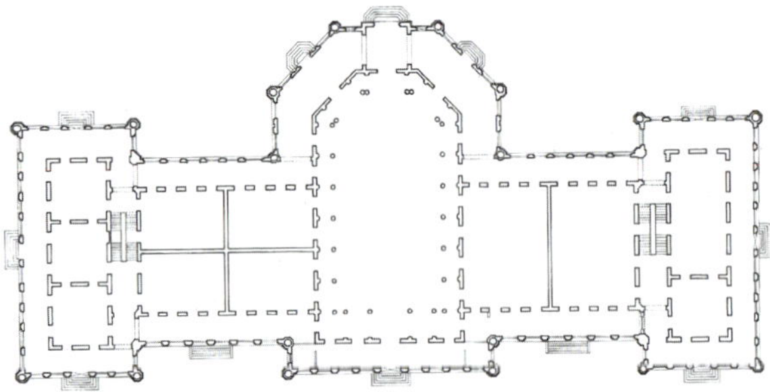

Plan

compensation for exile.... The dreariness, the expense, the remoteness of the station were sufficient to make it abhorrent to most Englishmen whose lot was placed in India."

There was considerable investment in the city's infrastructure, including the garbage disposal system, the waterworks, electric streetlights, the drainage system, and road improvements. And, a significant number of buildings were created in the Ramna area for official, educational, and residential purposes. The two most architecturally ambitious edifices built here were Curzon Hall (presently the Science Faculty of the University of Dhaka), named after the incumbent Viceroy Lord Curzon, who laid the foundation of the building on February 14, 1904, and the Government House (now the Dhaka High Court).

Ahmad Hasan Dani, author of *Dacca: A Record of Its Changing Fortunes* (1956), claimed that Curzon Hall was originally built as a town hall for the colonial administration.

Curzon Hall: loggias

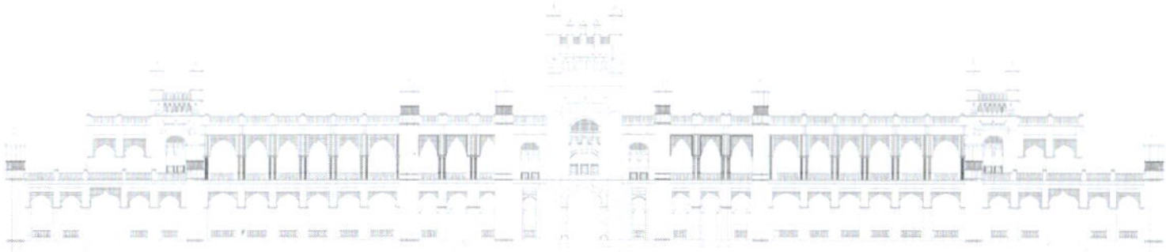

Front elevation

But, according to historian Sharif Uddin Ahmed, the building was constructed as a library for Dhaka College. The provenance of the building remains contested. Funding for Curzon Hall was provided by the zamindar princes of Bhawal, an estate in the eastern district of Dhaka, in British Bengal. They contributed taka 1,50,000 for the construction of the red brick edifice at Ramna. Their motivation was twofold: They were eager to be affiliated with Lord Curzon's development programs for the new capital, and the self-promotion would enhance their visibility and esteem.

The two-story building represents a hybrid style of European and Indian architectural forms and elements—known variously as Indo-European or Indo-Saracenic—that was popular around the turn of the century in colonial India. Contemporaneous buildings elsewhere in India, such as the Taj Mahal Hotel in Mumbai (architect: W. A. Chambers; 1903) and Howrah Station in Kolkata (architect: Halsey Ricardo;

Exterior façade details

Latticework detail

1900–1908), exhibit a similar blending of architectural styles. Synthesizing imperial grandiosity with sporadic Mughal motifs, the imposing building symbolizes how the colonial administration sought to include elements of "local" architecture as a way to show its sensitivity to native culture, which they hoped would counter growing nationalist sentiments among the natives.

While Curzon Hall's plan demonstrates European spatial sensitivity, its red brick exterior—adorned with multicusped arches, projected eaves, continuous loggias, brackets, lattices, corner turrets, and kiosks (*chattis*)—evokes images of Mughal architecture. A typical Mughal building motif, the kiosk defines the skyline of Curzon Hall, as it had at Humayun's tomb and Red Fort, in Delhi; the Taj Mahal and the

Front façade

tomb of Itmad-ud-Daulah, in Agra; and the Diwan-i-Khas at Fatehpur Sikri, in Agra. Like Itmad-ud-Daulah's tomb, Curzon Hall's balustrade features decorative *jali* (intricate ornamental latticework) and rises above a bracketed cornice. A continuous verandah wraps around the building, providing a recessed area and protecting the inner rooms from the penetrating monsoon rains.

The composition of the north-facing building is symmetrical: A grand central hall is flanked by linear wings on either side, terminated by rectangular building forms. The colonnaded three-story central hall is the focus of the plan and accessible from all sides. Loggias wrap the interior of the hall on the second and third floors. Colorful square panels adorn the ceiling.

The entrance is marked by a lofty projecting tower that appears to have compensated for the absence of a dome. The tower has three tall horseshoe windows, framed within an arched niche. Soaring kiosks crown the tower on four corners, with three smaller kiosks in between on each side. Curzon Hall is not an extraordinary building, but its elevation—variegated by pilasters, bays, panels, arched windows, eaves, and kiosks—presents a delightful impression. Rising from Ramna's lush, foliated garden, it reveals a quiet grandeur.

5. FACULTY OF FINE ARTS

LOCATION: University of Dhaka, Kazi Nazrul Islam Avenue, Dhaka 1000
ARCHITECT: Muzharul Islam
CONSTRUCTION: 1953–1955

PRACTICAL INFORMATION:

Visitors to the Faculty of Fine Arts do not need permission to see the outside of the building. Permission is required to enter the building.

Contact:
Office of the Registrar
Administrative Building (2nd Floor)
University of Dhaka, Dhaka 1000

Phone: +88-02-9670531/4020
E-Mail: registrar@du.ac.bd

5 Faculty of Fine Arts
6 Teacher–Student Center (TSC)
9 Department of Architecture Building
14 Priyo Prangan Apartment Complex
18 Museum of Independence and Independence Monument

NEARBY ATTRACTIONS:

A Begum Sufia Kamal National Public Library
B Bangladesh National Museum

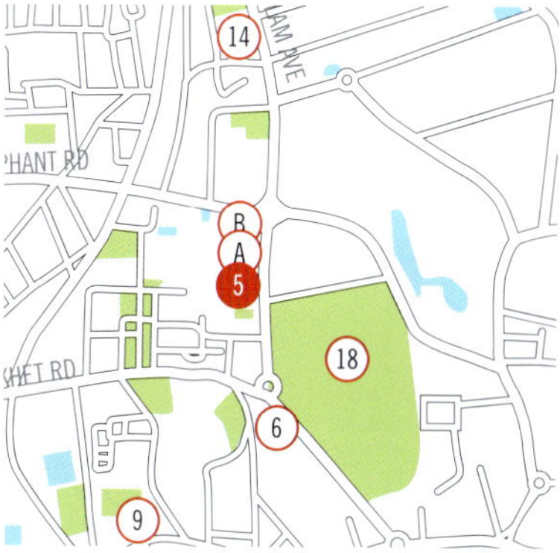

Designed by the pioneering Bengali architect Muzharul Islam (1923–2012), the Faculty of Fine Arts signaled the beginning of Bengali modernism in the architecture of East Pakistan, now Bangladesh. Located on the northern edge of the University of Dhaka campus, the Faculty of Fine Arts exemplifies a trendsetting building in which the tenets of Modern architecture mesh with the climatic and organizational needs of a tropical region. The result is a remarkable architectural ensemble—comprising administrative offices, faculty rooms, classrooms, art studios, and student common rooms—nestled in an urban garden. Muzharul Islam's education in the East and the West afforded him a nuanced perspective that, in turn, helped transcend parochial Islamic nationalism and elitist adulation of the West, conflicting sentiments that divided the political landscape of Pakistan in the wake of the Indian Partition in 1947.

Muzharul Islam was the first professionally trained local architect in East Pakistan. Born in the Murshidabad district, in West Bengal, Islam's childhood was spent in a multicultural and multifaith environment. This life-shaping experience arguably fostered the humanist ethos that framed his aesthetic persona. He attended Calcutta University from 1940 to 1942 and received a Bachelor of Science degree. A few years later, Islam went to Bengal Engineering College at Shibpur, in West Bengal, where he was awarded a Bachelor of Engineering (civil engineering) degree, in 1946. After the Indian Partition, his family moved to East Bengal, which became East Pakistan, where he joined the Pakistan Public Works Department (PWD) as an engineer.

While employed at the PWD, Muzharul Islam was awarded a scholarship to study architecture at the University of Oregon in the United States. He received his Bachelor of Architecture degree from that university in 1952. Later, during the 1950s and early 1960s, he attended the Architectural Association, in London, and Yale University, in the United States, respectively, and earned post-professional degrees in architecture. While at Yale, Islam was fortunate to know some of the prevailing luminaries of American architecture, namely, Paul Rudolph and Louis Kahn. He later collaborated with them and acted as their local mentor when they were designing buildings in Bangladesh, during the 1960s. In fact, Muzharul Islam was instrumental in inviting

Courtyard

Gallery with louvers

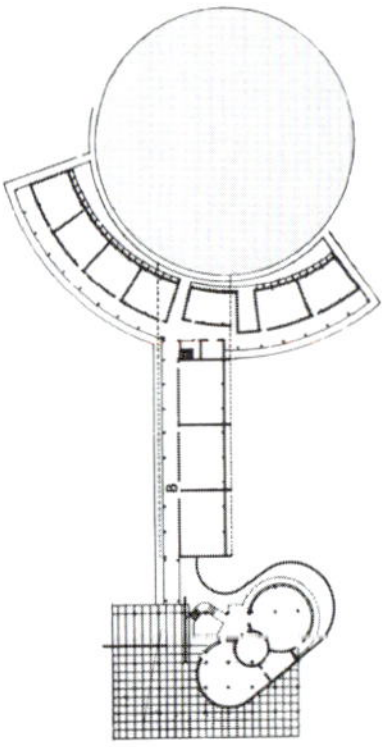
Ground floor plan

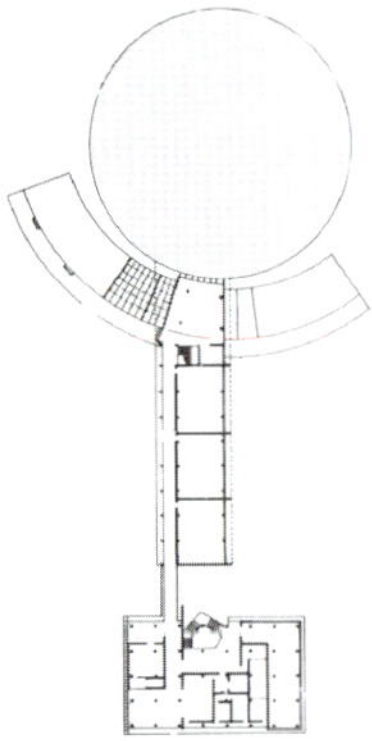
1st floor plan

Louis Kahn to design the National Assembly building (also known as the Parliament building), in Dhaka, on behalf of the Government of Pakistan.

Before setting up his own architectural practice, Islam served as Senior Architect of the Provincial Government of East Pakistan (1958–1964). Muzharul Islam is credited with introducing modernist aesthetics to a postcolonial country in which public architecture was marked mostly by a hybrid of colonial and provincial Mughal styles, or blandly utilitarian corridor-and-room building boxes. A staunch socialist and secularist, Islam's architectural oeuvre expresses a romantic faith in an architect's capacity to positively influence society. For him, architecture was no less a form of cultural activism. While embodying the heroic idealism of mid-20th-century Modern architecture, Islam refused to accept the perceived schism of the European Enlightenment and a Bengali consciousness—somewhat in the vein of the poet and Nobel Laureate Rabindranath Tagore.

Courtyard

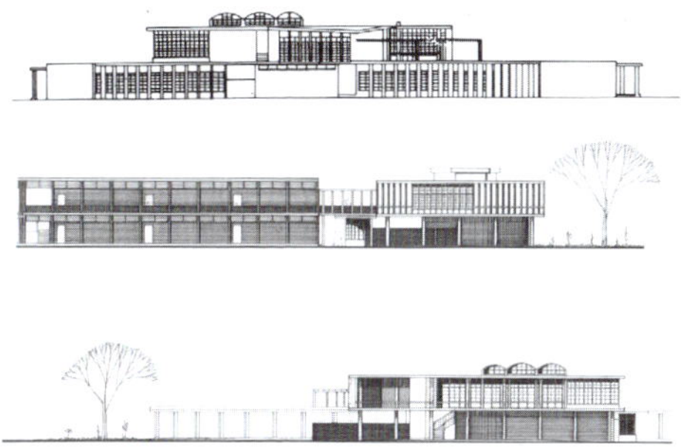

Sections and elevations

Islam spearheaded the creation of a respectable architectural profession in a country that was either dominated by expatriate architects, or steeped in a technocratic bureaucracy that saw civil engineering as the legitimate profession of the building industry. During the two decades following the Indian Partition, Muzharul Islam's designs for the Faculty of Fine Arts, the University of Dhaka Library (1953), the Road Research Institute and Laboratories (1964), and the National Institute of Public Administration building (1964–1969) collectively created the critical mass of Modern buildings that strengthened the view of architecture as a respectable career pursuit.

Muzharul Islam designed the Faculty of Fine Arts immediately after returning from the United States in 1952. Marion Dean Ross, his architectural history professor at the University of Oregon, introduced him to the key figures of Modern architecture, as well as to the regional architecture of California and Oregon. A well-known architectural historian, Ross sensitized him to the social

Faculty of Fine Arts: courtyard stairs

purposes of Modern architecture. Upon returning home, Muzharul Islam found it imperative to search for a modern Bengali identity in architecture, a particularly poignant mission in the politically heated atmosphere of the Language Movement in East Pakistan. (Bengalis refused to accept Urdu, the primary language in West Pakistan, as the only state language.)

A visitor's first encounter with the Faculty of Fine Arts provides the tentative impression of a Bengali version of Le Corbusier's Villa Savoye. A host of nuanced architectural modulations and environmental adaptations reveal how Muzharul Islam's work informs a modernist architectural language with self-conscious considerations of climatic needs and local building materials, particularly exposed brick. Unlike the Franco-Swiss architect's masterpiece in a suburb of Paris, where pilotis lift up a ribbon-windowed white box, here they raise an open pavilion formed by two sleek flat slabs. The pavilion on the second floor includes a spacious terrace, a teacher's room, and the girls' common room. Vertical wooden louvers on the south side connect the two flat slabs of the pavilion. These louvers temper the fierce tropical sun in the afternoon and channel the southern breeze, creating a gallery space or a sort of tropical piano nobile, overlooking the busy street to the east and green courtyard to the south.

The ground floor entry, flanked on one side by two circular exhibition spaces, provides a fluid gateway to an oasis-like

Bengali New Year's Parade

urban enclave, a rarity in an extremely populous city with an acute shortage of open spaces. Beyond the entry block, visitors discover a remarkable set of low-rise and sprawling buildings, all blending with the green around them.

Beyond the entrance is an evocative courtyard, awash in reflected light from all sides, especially the brick wall on the west. This little *maidan* (open space) in Muzharul Islam's Faculty of Fine Arts conjures up the archetypal image of the courtyard as the social hub in a Bengali rural homestead. Spatially, the courtyard connects the entry pavilion with the linear academic building that runs along the east-west axis. Yet, the courtyard is also where the visitor experiences the tour de force of Islam's architectural design, its *genius loci* (spirit of place). The key features of the courtyard are a sculptural concrete staircase, which brings a kinetic quality to the space surrounding it; the leafy tree at the middle of the courtyard; and the brick screen wall that frames its spatial experience. The two-story academic wing takes maximum advantage of the southern breeze. This wing intersects with an arc of studios that were supposed to overlook a circular pond. However, the pond has never been realized.

The entire architectural ensemble is nestled in a calm, verdant urban meadow. A sensibly conceived relationship between indoor and outdoor spaces creates the academic ambiance necessary for studying the arts. Muzharul Islam incorporated the original vegetation and an image of the local landscape into his design, capturing the spirit of place through the visual language of his building. The spatial experience of the Faculty of Fine Arts gives the impression that it is environmentally rooted in Shahbagh—which means "royal garden"—the name of this area of Dhaka.

Today, the Faculty of Fine Arts has become an icon not only of art education in the country, but also of its modernist national aspiration. The much-celebrated cultural procession on April 14, the first day of the Bengali calendar, begins here. Art students create giant papier-mâché masks, birds, animals, and fish, which symbolize Bengal's agro-pastoral heritage. These mascots are carried in the parade that traverses the city streets. This annual event is one of the most colorful urban phenomena to behold in the month of April.

6. TEACHER–STUDENT CENTER (TSC)

LOCATION: University of Dhaka, Suhrawardi Udyan Road, Dhaka 1000
ARCHITECT: Constantinos Apostolos Doxiadis
CONSTRUCTION: 1962

PRACTICAL INFORMATION:

Visitors to the Teacher–Student Center (TSC) do not need permission to see the building.

Here are more resources for information about the TSC:
Phone: +88-02-9661900

URL: www.du.ac.bd/home/office_and_admin/tsc

1 Lalbagh Fort Complex
4 Curzon Hall
5 Faculty of Fine Arts
6 Teacher–Student Center (TSC)
9 Department of Architecture Building
18 Museum of Independence and Independence Monument.

NEARBY ATTRACTIONS:

A University of Dhaka Library (Architect: Muzharul Islam)
B Faculty of Business Studies, University of Dhaka (formerly NIPA Building; Architect: Muzharul Islam)

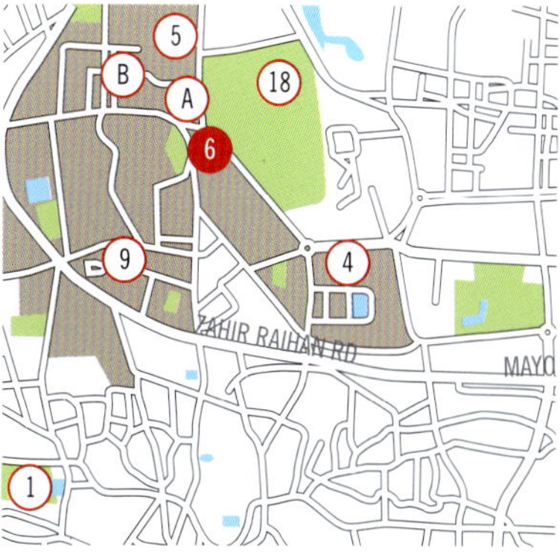

The Greek architect, planner, and theoretician Constantinos Apostolos Doxiadis (1913–1975) designed the University of Dhaka's Teacher–Student Center (TSC) during the early 1960s. This was a turbulent time, marked by conflicting currents of political anxiety and architectural optimism in what was then East Pakistan. Despite the rising tension between the two wings of Pakistan, many architectural opportunities arose in East Pakistan between 1958 and 1968, the so-called Decade of Development that benefited from the United States' technical assistance to Pakistan.

The United States allied with Pakistan as part of its Cold War-era foreign policy to create a geostrategic buffer against the socialist milieu of the Soviet Union–India axis in South Asia. Under the purview of a technical assistance program, the United States Agency for International Development (USAID) and the Ford Foundation provided support for building educational and civic institutions in East Pakistan. (USAID was created in 1961, during the presidency of John F. Kennedy.) Since there was a dearth of experienced architects in East Pakistan, the government sought the services of American and European architects for a host of buildings that were constructed during the 1960s. Among these architects were Doxiadis, Richard Vrooman, Daniel C. Dunham, Paul Rudolph, Stanley Tigerman, Richard Neutra, and Robert G. Boughey.

Doxiadis designed multiple institutional complexes, sponsored by the Ford Foundation. Among them were the Bangladesh Academy for Rural Development, in Comilla; College of Home Economics, in Dhaka; and the Institute of Education and Research, University of Dhaka. However, it was the TSC that became one of the emblems of Dhaka's architectural modernity. Located at the historic heart of the University of Dhaka, TSC exemplifies a modernist architectural sensitivity toward spatial needs for tropical climatic conditions. It blends local parameters of space-making—particularly the indoor-outdoor continuum and generation of space around courtyards—with the International Style's visual expression of building forms.

To gain a deeper understanding of the TSC, it helps to explore the architect's personal development. Doxiadis was born in 1913, in Bulgaria, of Greek parents. Early in his childhood, he was influenced by his father, who was the Greek Minister

Student Union Building

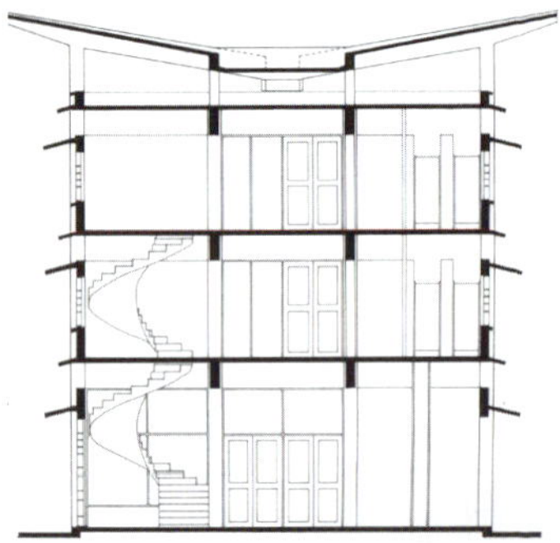

Section

of Refugees, Social Welfare, and Public Health. In 1935, Doxiadis graduated from the Athens Technical University as an Architect-Engineer, and a year later, he earned his Doctorate at the Charlottenburg University, in Berlin. Subsequently, he served as Chief Town Planning Officer for Greater Athens and, during World War II, as Head of the Department of Regional and Town Planning at the Ministry of Public Works. After the war, he became the Director-General of the Ministry of Housing and Reconstruction. In 1951, he founded Doxiadis Associates, a private consulting firm of engineers, architects, and planners. The firm's rapid growth led to offices on five continents and projects in 40 countries.

Doxiadis created the Athens Center of Ekistics in 1963, although he had introduced the concept of ekistics during the 1930s. As he later explained in his book *Ekistics: An Introduction to the Science of Human Settlements* (1968), the term represented an objective, comprehensive, and integrative approach to all principles

Master plan

and theories of human settlements. Criticizing the top-down planning model of the first half of the 20th century, Doxiadis employed the notion of ekistics to promote a multidisciplinary, inclusive, and bottom-up approach to architecture and city planning. He hoped that such a method would create a synergy among the organic context of the locale, data-driven theorization of planning, and universal values of harmonious living.

It is evident that Doxiadis tried out his theories of ekistics at the TSC, among other projects in Bangladesh. Construction of the Teacher–Student Center complex began in March 1962, after the University of Dhaka authorities gave their approval of Doxiadis Associates' final design. The site comprises 1.5 ha (3.7 acres) at the intersection of Bakshi Bazar Road and Mymensing Road, with the Suhrawardi Udyan (park) on the east. Access to the site is from the north, where three streets meet to form a major urban node and the geographic center of the sprawling campus of the University of Dhaka. It is a historic gathering place for students and the public during such national celebrations as Liberation Day, Independence Day, Language Movement Day, and Pohela Boishakh (the first day of the Bengali year). The horizontal building block to the north acts as a transition from the urban hustle and bustle to the verdant interior of the complex.

Doxiadis conceived TSC as an architectural ensemble, comprising six elements: (1) the Student Union Building, which accommodates the student union headquarters, offices for students and teachers, conference rooms, a library, lounges, bookshops, and a general store; (2) the

Courtyard

Hallway

auditorium, which serves as a multipurpose hall and features a seating capacity of 800; (3) the cafeteria; (4) the guest house; (5) the swimming pool; and (6) the water tower (unbuilt).

The buildings are aligned with the east-west axis, to take advantage of the prevailing breeze from the south or north. The three-story Student Union Building is rectangular in plan, 48.16 m by 11.28 m (158 ft. by 37 ft.), and composed of a reinforced concrete frame and non-loadbearing brick walls. It is a trendsetting building as the structure employs a double roof to minimize heat gain, by allowing the cool breeze to pass through the two layers of the roof. Providing a protective canopy for the building shell, the upper roof has a wing-like formation, with rainwater drainage in between.

The auditorium, also rectangular in plan, is 51.82 m by 25.91 m (170 ft. by 85 ft.) and is covered by a reinforced concrete parabolic vault, a pioneering construction technique in the country. The auditorium has a level floor, with removable seating, and a spacious stage, with dressing rooms. The airy cafeteria features a high ceiling and overlooks the sprawling courtyard to the north. It consists of two segments placed on either side of a linear green mall. The west wing of the cafeteria contains a large game room, plus dressing rooms, showers, and toilets that serve the swimming pool. The east wing houses the main eating area and a kitchen, with the customary auxiliary spaces. The hypostyle hall of the cafeteria has a reinforced concrete frame and provides a continuous band of clerestory around its perimeter. The guest house, east of the cafeteria, comprises six rooms, each with an attached bathroom and balcony.

Covered walkways, supported on steel columns, weave together the major buildings and green spaces. Functioning more like a continuous loop of linear pavilions, rather than corridors, the walkways are the social spine of the entire complex. The Teacher–Student Center is one of the first buildings in Bangladesh to employ a pavilion theme in non-residential architecture.

Considered a sensible response to the needs of a tropical climate, Doxiadis assembled the buildings and courtyards in a lush tapestry of organic fluidity and spatial

Cafeteria

interconnectivity. The whole complex feels like a miniature city, perhaps, offering a spatial program (although in a much smaller scale) antithetical to the recently completed projects of Le Corbusier's Chandigarh or Lucio Costa and Oscar Niemeyer's Brasilia.

Over the years, TSC has become part of a national narrative. Many of the pivotal student movements took shape around this historic urban node. Furthermore, TSC is also celebrated as a verdant and breezy urban space, a rare liberating experience in this overcrowded city.

Entry hall

7. KAMALAPUR RAILWAY STATION

LOCATION: Kamalapur Road, Dhaka 1222
ARCHITECTS: Daniel C. Dunham and Robert G. Boughey
CONSTRUCTION: 1961–1968

PRACTICAL INFORMATION:

Kamalapur Railway Station operates 24 hours a day, 7 days a week

URL: www.railway.gov.bd

7 Kamalapur Railway Station
12 Bangladesh Chemical Industries Corporation (BCIC) Headquarters

NEARBY ATTRACTION:

A Notre Dame College (Architect: Robert G. Boughey)

The first railway line in East Bengal—connecting Kolkata with the western Bangladeshi town of Kushtia—was introduced in 1862. Called the Eastern Bengal Railway, this expansion of train service to East Bengal signaled a new phase in the growth of the region's colonial economy. However, the province east of the Padma River, including such urban centers as Dhaka, Chittagong, and Sylhet, long remained deprived of the benefits of railway because the extensive river system of the deltaic country created geographic logistical issues.

Even by 1885, the only railway line on the eastern side of the Padma was the one connecting Dhaka and the northern town of Mymensingh. Still considered a provincial town at that time, Dhaka's railway infrastructure was nominal. The railway station constructed at Phulbaria, demarcating the northern extent of Dhaka, only served the people in and around the urban area. It was a rudimentary facility with one platform, a small yard, and a locomotive shed. The railway line leading to Phulbaria formed a semicircular northern barrier of the city. However, the train track did not affect the flow of vehicular traffic to and from the area because the city's total traffic volume was rather small.

During the early 20th century, Dhaka's urban status rose, and its economy grew, even more so after 1947, when it became the provincial capital of East Pakistan. The existing railway line bifurcated the capital into the old city and the new city, expanding northward. The north-south traffic flow was severely hampered because the existing train lines converging at the Phulbaria Railway Station cut roads at various points.

The most reasonable remedy was to shift the Phulbaria Station and divert the railway lines to a less populated and sparsely used area, thus easing the north-south vehicular movement without much hindrance. Furthermore, this move would help unify the old city and the new city. Accordingly, in 1948, experts suggested that the railway station be resituated to its present location at Kamalapur. However, the proposal came to fruition only a decade later, in 1958, when the provincial government was entrusted with executing the plan. The train line was diverted from Tejgaon to Khilgaon and then to Kamalapur, removing the previous east-west barrier that cut through the middle of the growing city.

The inauguration of the new railway station at Kamalapur on April 27, 1968,

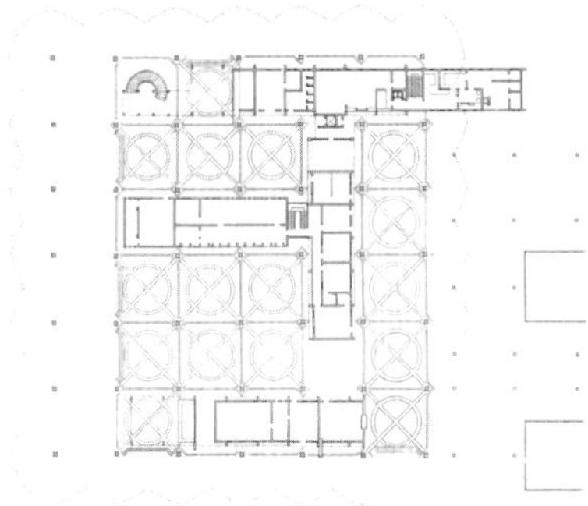

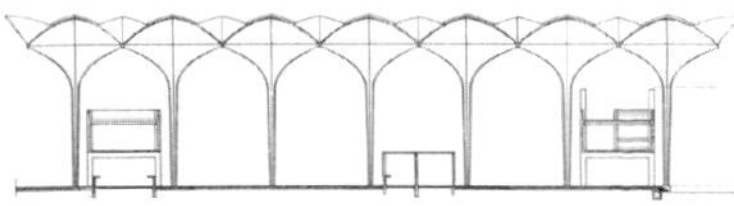

Plan

Elevation

introduced a new chapter in the history of railway transportation in East Pakistan, now Bangladesh. Not only was it the largest modern railway station in the country, but it also embodied the modernist spirit in architecture that defined the decade of the 1960s. The key buildings of the station and the yard occupy about 63.13 ha (156 acres) of land in the southeast region of Dhaka. The sprawling complex includes new railway lines, access roads, staff quarters, and various other amenities for railway passengers. There are 10 platforms, 11 booking counters, and multiple passenger lounges.

The architects of the Kamalapur Railway Station were two Americans: Daniel C. Dunham and Robert G. Boughey. They came to Dhaka as employees of Louis Berger & Consulting Engineers (PAK) Ltd., a multinational architectural and engineering consortium with headquarters in America and West Pakistan. Founded in 1953 by Dr. Louis Berger, Louis Berger & Associates undertook many infrastructural projects around the globe. While

working in Dhaka as a design consultant for the firm, Dunham (the adopted son of a Nebraska couple and a Harvard graduate) was hired to teach architecture at the East Pakistan University of Engineering and Technology (EPUET; renamed BUET, following the independence of Bangladesh), in which the newly minted architecture program was led by USAID-sponsored professors from the Texas A&M University faculty, including Richard Vrooman. The Pennsylvania-born Robert Boughey was trained as an architect at New York's Pratt Institute (where he also taught in the late 1960s) and the Architectural Association, in London. Since 1973, Boughey has managed a thriving architectural practice in Bangkok, Thailand. There, he won many architectural design contracts, including the Bangkok Art and Culture Centre.

At Kamalapur, Dunham and Boughey's design challenge was to create a wide-span structure that would synthesize the language of Modern architecture with the requirements of a tropical climate. The official demands to incorporate Islamic building iconography in the railway station's design complicated their task. The result, however, is the unusual concrete roof structure of the train terminal, with a parasol roof that shelters an interconnected series of low-rise structures. The profile of the terminal—a rhythmic pattern of gently pointed and arched concrete shells—evokes a typical image of tropical conditions, in which an umbrella provides protection from the monsoon rains. The design creates a light-filled and cross-ventilated train terminal, reminiscent of Mughal pavilions, with deeply recessed spatial volumes.

The thin-shelled concrete canopy at Kamalapur reflects the prior experience of both architects. As a student at Harvard, Dunham designed structures with shell concrete. The government agency in charge of the terminal's construction was understandably anxious because of the unusual composition material of the proposed terminal. At Boughey's suggestion, a smaller version of the terminal was constructed to study the structural feasibility of the project. Berger's Stanley Jewkes, an experienced engineer who recently oversaw the construction of large-scale concrete structures in Malaysia, served as the project engineer.

The square plan of the terminal contains six square bays on each side. Forty-nine columns support 36 cusped shells that rise to a height of 17.98 m (59 ft.). The columns widen as they rise, splitting into four ribs that create the diagonal square grid of the roof system. The concrete roof structure provides a rhythmic visual effect, unifying the spaces below it. The parabolic roofline recalls other contemporary masterpieces, such as Danish architect Jorn Utzon's Sydney Opera House (1957–1973). Just as Utzon's Opera House shaped the skyline of the Sydney harbor, Kamalapur Railway Station's repetitive arches created a new skyline in this low-rise area of the city. Other contemporaneous iconic roof structures that might have inspired Kamalapur were Eero Saarinen's Trans World Airlines Flight Center (1956–1962) at the John F. Kennedy International Airport in New York and a number of parabolic structures in Lucio Costa and Oscar Niemeyer's Brasilia.

The design of the Kamalapur Railway Station organizes various functional spaces, such as ticket booths, administrative offices, passenger lounges, and waiting areas, under one unifying canopy roof. There are no internal divisions between function types. The entire architectural ensemble consists of two systems: the parabolic roof structure above and low-rise (one- and two-story) flat-roofed structures below it. Thus, the ambiance of the whole terminal is of a free-flowing, democratic public place, accessible from all sides. A circular, sculptural staircase in one corner grid provides vertical connections to the upper levels. Long concrete vaults with elevations lower than the terminal superstructure provide a covered platform for arriving and departing passengers.

The completion of the Kamalapur Railway Station was hailed as a landmark government accomplishment. Pakistan's President Muhammad Ayub Khan attended the opening ceremony. Commemorative stamps were even issued to celebrate the new terminal. Today, the parasol roof of the Kamalapur Railway Station continues to provide a unique skyline. It is a gateway that symbolizes the architectural energy defining the urban persona of the city. The station also serves as a transition point through which impoverished rural migrants enter the city of "big dreams." As much as it is an icon of the city's modernist architectural heritage, ironically, it transforms into a nighttime refuge for the city's less-fortunate inhabitants. More than any other building, this architectural masterpiece today presents many social commentaries on the city's grinding life.

8. NATIONAL ASSEMBLY BUILDING (JATIYO SHANGSHAD BHABAN)

LOCATION: Shangshad Bhaban, Manik Mia Avenue, Sher-e-Banglanagar, Dhaka 1207
ARCHITECT: Louis I. Kahn
SITE ARCHITECTS: Roy Vollmer, Gus Langford, and Henry Wilcots
CONSTRUCTION: 1964–1983
AWARD: Aga Khan Award for Architecture, 1987

PRACTICAL INFORMATION:

Visitors may pre-arrange a 4-hour guided tour of the National Assembly Building (also known as the Parliament building). There is an entry fee. See "Facts for the Visitor," p. 159, for details.

8 National Assembly Building (Jatiyo Shangshad Bhaban)
10 Bangladesh Agricultural Research Council (BARC) Headquarters
19 Krishibid Institution of Bangladesh (KIB)

NEARBY ATTRACTIONS:

A St. Joseph Higher Secondary School (Architect: Robert G. Boughey)
B Shaheed Suhrawardy Medical College and Hospital (Architect: Louis I. Kahn)

The American architect Louis Isadore Kahn's National Assembly building (also known as the Parliament building and Jatiyo Shangshad Bhaban) in Dhaka is one of the celebrated icons of 20th-century architecture. Intriguingly, Kahn was not the first choice for the project. After Le Corbusier and Alvar Aalto had turned down the invitation from the Government of Pakistan, the megaproject went to the architect from Philadelphia. Following multiple design iterations and many bureaucratic entanglements, the construction of the capitol building for the provincial capital of Dhaka began in October 1964, at Sher-e-Banglanagar. Its conceptualization and construction parallels the nationalist struggle of the people of East Pakistan, which emerged as the independent nation of Bangladesh in 1971.

Louis Khan was born in Russian-controlled Estonia in 1901 of Jewish parents. He immigrated to America with his mother and siblings in 1906 (his father had arrived two years before them) and grew up in an itinerant household in northeastern Philadelphia, a predominantly Jewish area. Although the family had limited resources, it was not surprising that Kahn's artistic talents would lead him to study architecture. Trained in the Beaux-Arts method, he received a Bachelor of Architecture degree from the University of Pennsylvania in 1924. In the 1950s, his designs for Yale University Art Gallery and Design Center and Alfred Newton Richards Medical Research Building and Biology Building (now David Goddard Laboratories, located at his alma mater), drew worldwide attention.

Kahn was an admired professor of architecture at the University of Pennsylvania and Yale. At Yale, his paths crossed with the Bangladeshi architect Muzharul Islam, when the latter was studying there from 1960 to 1961. Muzharul Islam was inspired by the charismatic teacher, and he played an instrumental role in bringing Kahn to Bangladesh.

Kahn first visited Dhaka in early March of 1963, after he had received the commission to plan the Parliament complex of East Pakistan. The decade of the 1960s was a politically tumultuous period in East Pakistan. The people of East Pakistan felt exploited and ignored by West Pakistan's military regime and, consequently, dreamed of independence from the doomed political geography of a nation with two populations separated by more than 1,609 km (1,000 mi.). Aware of the political and economic disparity between the two halves

Parliament hostels

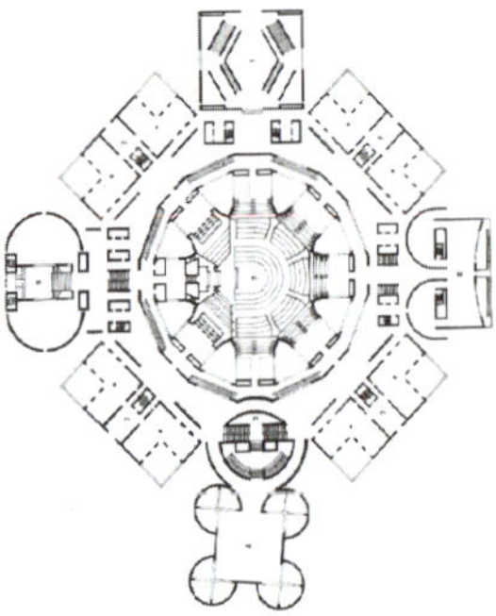

Ground floor plan

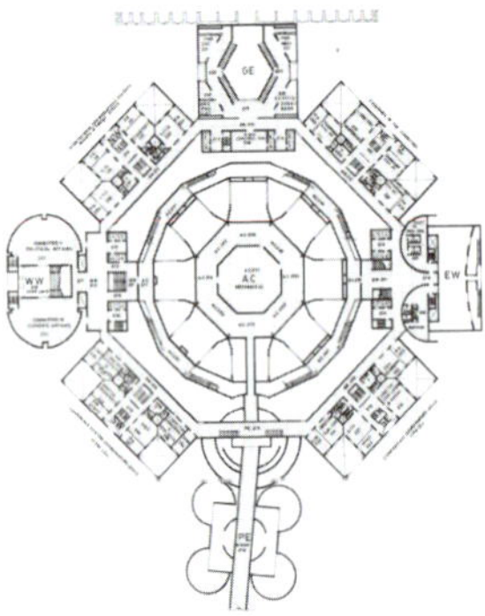

Upper floor plan

of Pakistan and concerned about his own reelection bid, Ayub Khan's administration came up with the clever idea of a "second capital" for East Pakistan.

The political drama that ensued explains how the National Assembly building, first conceived as a "bribe" for the Bengalis, gradually took on an entirely new identity as a symbol of the people's struggle for self-rule. With rudimentary construction tools and bamboo scaffolding tied with crude jute ropes, approximately 2,000 lungi-saree-clad construction workers erected a monumental government building. If the Shahid Minar symbolized the Language Movement during the 1950s, then the National Assembly building portrayed the rise of the independence-minded Bengalis during the 1960s.

In his design, Kahn searched for inspiration from the Bengal delta; its rivers; green pastoral, expansive landscape; raised homesteads; and land-water geography. Soon after he had first arrived in Dhaka, he traveled by boat along the Buriganga River and sketched scenes to

Parliament building from south plaza

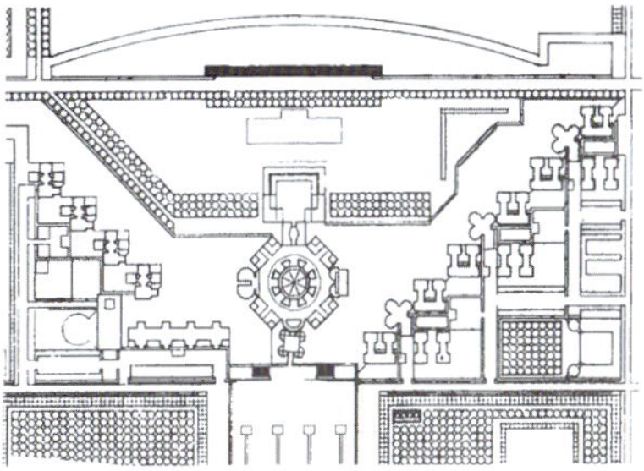

Site plan

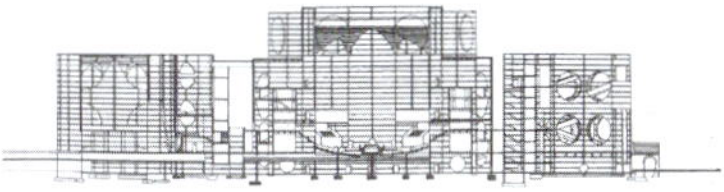

Section

understand life in this tropical land. He didn't have any problems blending Bengali vernacular impressions with those of the classical Greco-Roman and Egyptian architecture that he had studied thoroughly during the 1950s.

As the war broke out on March 25, 1971, Kahn's field office in East Pakistan quickly closed, and construction work discontinued. The work resumed after the independence of Bangladesh. When it was completed in 1983—nine years after Kahn's unexpected death in New York City—the Parliament complex emblematized the political odyssey of a people to statehood.

The focus of the capitol site (404.69 ha or 1,000 acres)—aligned on a north-south city axis—is the seven-story diamond-shaped National Assembly building, wrapped in 41.15 m (135 ft.) high concrete walls. There are two adjoining plazas. Facing the city, the south plaza was designed as a public entrance. To the north, marble-clad Presidential Plaza was designated as a ceremonial entrance. At present, visitors enter the site from the east, via an internal

road that meets the grade-level causeway perpendicularly.

Eight freestanding building masses surround the National Assembly building's ambulatory, which then encloses the 16-sided, 500 seat assembly chamber, the central rotunda of the octagonal building. The parliamentary heart of the country's political system, the assembly chamber hosts the 300 Members of the Parliament (MP) of the unicameral legislative body. The interior of the building—particularly the somewhat labyrinthine 25.91 m (85 ft.) high ambulatory—is a tour de force of architectural imagination.

Remaining open to the elements for many years, eventually, a roof was designed for the assembly chamber, 17.07 m (56 ft.) radius in plan. After many proposals, the final roof design consisted of a series of parabolic concrete shells that create eight large clerestory apertures, admitting soft light into the chamber. To the eyes of many visitors, the assembly chamber is reminiscent of the Pantheon's interior, which fascinated Kahn.

The exterior of the building features bold triangular, rectangular, circular, and semicircular cutouts, which were framed within horizontal marble bands every 1.52 m (5 ft.) on the façade. According to some sources, it is a module established by the maximum feasible amount of concrete that could be poured manually each day. By incorporating horizontal marble strips, Kahn could mitigate any potential difference in the hue and texture of the concrete pourings on different days. He also added

vertical marble strips with wider spacing, creating a comprehensive grid on the entire building, somewhat humanizing its scale. At the south entrance of the Parliament, the prayer hall—shaped by four towering cylindrical forms—is skewed slightly off axis to conform to the correct orientation toward Mecca. The building rises majestically from a geometrically shaped water body. This moat has popularly been interpreted as a reference to the deltaic landscape and riverine geography of Bangladesh. Diagonally flanking the Parliament building on the east and west are the two-story red brick hostels for the MPs and Community Halls.

Much has been written about the influence of both Western classical antiquity and Mughal planning on Kahn's design of the capitol project, as well as how his concerns for the tropical climate conditioned its multilayered forms. Historians generally agree that Kahn's Parliament complex is a sensible blending of modernist aesthetics with Greco-Roman gravitas and a spiritualized view of pastoral Bengal, where land, water, and the hut coexist with sublime simplicity.

Today, not only does the building embody the hopes and aspirations of the nation, but it also provides a much-needed urban oasis in a congested metropolis of 18 million people. The south plaza of the Parliament complex is off-limits to the public because of alleged security concerns. However, the wide sidewalks of Manik Mia Avenue, along the south periphery, offer a vibrant urban promenade where city-dwellers typically gather and socialize against the panoramic backdrop of Kahn's building.

9. DEPARTMENT OF ARCHITECTURE BUILDING

LOCATION: Bangladesh University of Engineering and Technology (BUET), Dhaka 1000
PRIMARY ARCHITECT: Richard Edwin Vrooman
LOCAL ARCHITECT: Mohammed Saber Jafar, Engineer
CONSTRUCTION: 1964

PRACTICAL INFORMATION:

Visitors to the Department of Architecture building can see the premises from the outside. Permission is required to enter the studios, which are open from 9 am to 5 pm, Saturday to Wednesday.

Contact:
Head, Department of Architecture
BUET
Dhaka 1000

Phone: +88-02-9665633

1 Lalbagh Fort Complex
4 Curzon Hall
5 Faculty of Fine Arts
6 Teacher-Student Center (TSC)
9 Department of Architecture Building
18 Museum of Independence and Independence Monument.

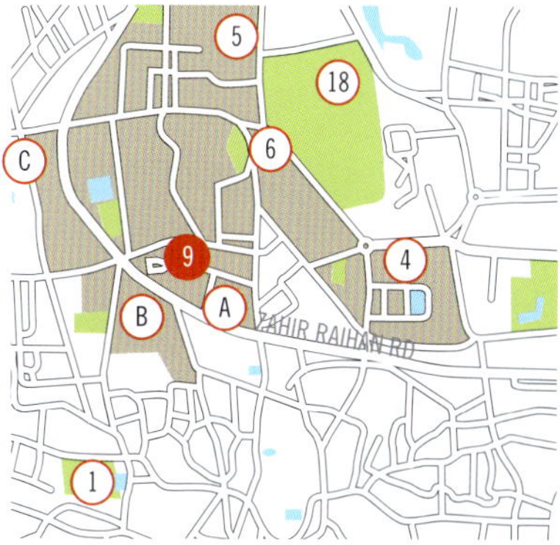

NEARBY ATTRACTIONS:

A Civil Engineering Building, BUET (Architect: Robert G. Boughey)
B Gymnasium and Student Dormitories, BUET (Titumir, Suhrawardy, and Sher-e-Bangla Halls; Architect: Robert G. Boughey)
C College of Home Economics (Architect: Constantinos Apostolos Doxiadis)

No building symbolizes the advent of professional architectural education in Bangladesh during the 1960s more appropriately than Richard "Dik" Vrooman's Department of Architecture building at the Bangladesh University of Engineering and Technology (BUET). An American architect and academic, Vrooman (1920–2002) took a leave of absence from his faculty position at Texas A&M University, spending the years 1961 through 1968 in Dhaka. Other Texas A&M professors who joined him included James C. Walden, Jr. (1962–1966) and Samuel T. Lanford (1963–1965).

They were brought to Dhaka through a partnership between the United States Agency for International Development (USAID) and Texas A&M, whose goal was to create a Department of Architecture at the East Pakistan University of Engineering and Technology (EPUET; renamed BUET after Bangladesh became an independent nation in 1971). The mission was to train local architects, filling the void of architectural design expertise necessitated by the burgeoning building industry, particularly between 1958 and 1968 during the so-called Decade of Development in Pakistan. Among the other expatriate architects who supported Vrooman and his colleagues were Daniel C. Dunham (1962–1967) and Jack R. Yardley (1966–1968), both of whom taught at the newly minted architecture program.

In 1961, during the presidency of John F. Kennedy, the U.S. Congress passed the Foreign Assistance Act, which sequestered military and non-military aid to foreign nations. Out of this legislation emerged USAID, designed to administer American economic and technical assistance to the developing nations of the world. Continuing the cooperation and exchange programs initiated under the International Cooperation Administration (ICA, 1955–1961), USAID's objective was to help these countries achieve their long-term economic and development goals. Pakistan received much assistance under this program, particularly in the education sector.

In 1962, the Government of Pakistan decided to upgrade Dhaka's Ahsanullah Engineering College to a full-fledged university, which became EPUET. The need for creating a Department of Architecture was urgently felt, particularly because there was a dearth of native architectural experts who could shoulder the task of designing various buildings alongside the handful of expatriate architects working in Pakistan.

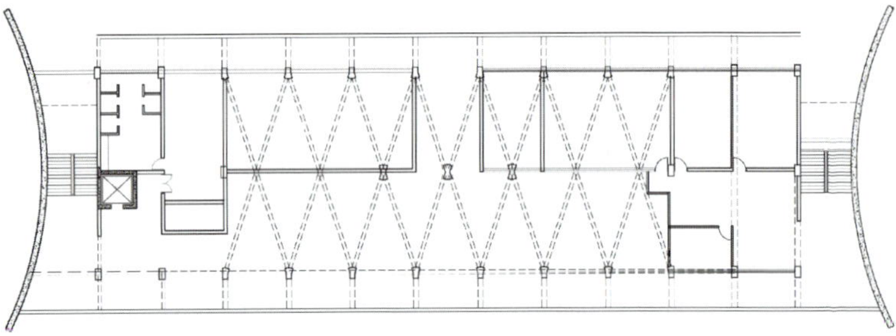

Ground floor plan

Overcoming many bureaucratic obstacles, Vrooman spearheaded the creation of an architecture program that would flourish rapidly. He became the first Dean of Architecture and designed its flagship building. By 1965, with four American teachers and 68 students at five levels, architecture grew rapidly as an academic discipline in East Pakistan. The construction of Vrooman's Department of Architecture building began in 1964, more or less contemporaneously with Louis Kahn's National Assembly building (also known as the Parliament building) in Dhaka. Engineer Mohammed Saber Jafar, a graduate of Bengal Engineering and Science University at Shibpur, West Bengal (now the Indian Institute of Engineering Science and Technology, Shibpur), served as the local architect for the project.

The Department of Architecture building at BUET is located at the northwestern edge of the campus on a wedge-shaped site. Two thoroughfares border the site to the north and south, intersecting in the west at Bakhshi Bazar. An internal campus road forms the eastern edge of the

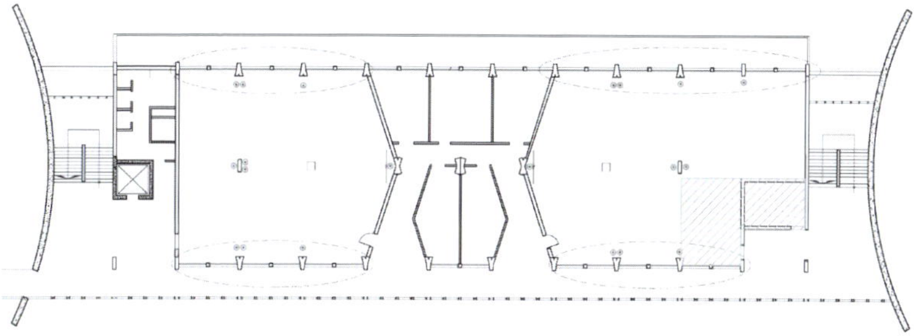

1st floor plan

site and provides access to the Architecture Faculty building complex. At the center of the triangular site was a large pond, which was later filled. Precast concrete pylons were inserted into the unstable soil to provide a secure building foundation. Architect Daniel C. Dunham proposed a master plan for this part of the campus, which was to include BUET's main library, auditorium, cafeteria, and teachers' club.

In the vein of Walter Gropius's Bauhaus in Dessau (1925–1926), Vrooman sought to design a building that would set a new paradigm for holistic academic environments in the country. His concept combined a four-story academic wing and a two-story administrative wing that were organized in an L-shape, offering functional clarity to the building program. The two rectangular arms of the L-shape and BUET's library help to form an appropriately scaled, lush green courtyard. The recessed corridors on all floors of the academic wing allow a continuous visual link to the courtyard.

This courtyard also connects to another paved courtyard adjoining the university's

cafeteria and auditorium. The academic wing includes all of the design studios, some faculty offices, a seminar room on the ground floor, and service areas. The administrative wing has a projecting vehicular porch that leads to a modest arrival hall. Adjacent to it are a reception area, staff offices, a jury space, and a teachers' lounge. On the southern edge of the administrative wing are the offices of the Head of the Architecture Department and the Dean of the Faculty. A double-height, covered outdoor space on the northern side of this wing serves as both a grand jury space and a concert theater. The second floor of this block houses the architecture library, computer center, and other auxiliary office spaces. On this level, overlooking the jury space, a bridge connects the two wings of the building.

The academic wing is rectangular in plan (approximately 61 m by 24.4 m or 200 ft. by 80 ft.), but features a diagonal beam system, creating a dynamic rhythm between the structure and the building envelope. The east-west axis of the volume allows for north-south cross ventilation and daylight. Studio spaces on the second, third, and fourth floors span the entire width of the building, creating an impression of an open-floor organization, which, in turn, helps foster a sense of academic community. At night, the illuminated building reveals its somewhat pixilated transparency to the surrounding campus.

The iconic features of the academic wing are the precast concrete louver panels, which serve as railings, while bringing light and air into the building. Each panel is 1.07 m (42 in.) wide and 2.44 m (96 in.) high and contains nine angled louvers. Between every two projecting floor beams there are four louver panels, hung at a mild angle to help temper the driving rain. As people approach the building from the east, the louvers collectively present the iconic persona of the building, a structural derivative of the brise-soleil theme that defines many of Le Corbusier's edifices. The louvered façade also invokes the Brutalist expression through exposed concrete and a building mass lifted off the ground by means of heavy piers.
For instance, one might be reminded of the patterned façade of Marcel Breuer's contemporaneous Department of Housing and Urban Development (HUD) in Washington, DC.

Elevation

Curved concrete walls on the east and west sides of the academic wing terminate the rectangular plan, while transcending the predictable box-like volume of institutional buildings found in the country. At the top of the curved wall, boldly projecting and centrally placed spouts collect rainwater and drain into circular ponds on the ground. Between the building shell and the curved wall are staircases at both ends. Smaller curved walls also support the vehicular porch and staircase on the west side of the administrative wing, providing an aesthetic theme for the entire ensemble.

The BUET site is far from Texas, where architect Vrooman taught and developed his professional practice, prior to coming to Bangladesh. Yet, in this unfamiliar territory, he created an edifice that beautifully blends with its climatic and cultural milieu. Making a suitable gesture to its tropical conditions, Vrooman's louvered building consciously blurs the boundary between inside and outside. It feels as though no other building could propel the journey of architectural education in this country more consciously than Vrooman's creation.

In recent times, additions have been made to the Department of Architecture building, somewhat compromising its original beauty. An ill-conceived "copycat" building for the Planning Department was constructed to the north, in the process, eliminating the sculptural ambience with which Vrooman's building once rose from a verdant base. Nonetheless, the courtyard of the Department of Architecture building has become a celebrated plaza that hosts a variety of festivals, attracting students and the public alike.

10. BANGLADESH AGRICULTURAL RESEARCH COUNCIL (BARC) HEADQUARTERS

LOCATION: Khamarbari Road, Farmgate, Dhaka 1215
ARCHITECT: Rabiul Hussain, of Shahidullah & Associates Ltd.
STRUCTURAL DESIGNER: Sheikh Mohammad Shaheedullah
CONSTRUCTION: 1978–1981

PRACTICAL INFORMATION:
Visitors to the Bangladesh Agricultural Research Council (BARC) headquarters should submit a request 7 days in advance. Premises are open from 9 am to 5 pm, Sunday to Thursday.

Contact:
Executive Chairman
Bangladesh Agricultural Research Council (BARC)
Farmgate, Dhaka 1215

Phone: +88-02-9135587 or +88-02-9110842

PABX: 9132214-18

E-Mail: ec-barc@barc.gov.bd or info@barc.gov.bd

8 National Assembly Building
(Jatiyo Shangshad Bhaban)
10 Bangladesh Agricultural Research Council (BARC)
19 Krishibid Institution of Bangladesh (KIB)

NEARBY ATTRACTIONS:

A Holy Rosary Church
B Bangabandhu Sheikh Mujibur Rahman Novo Theatre

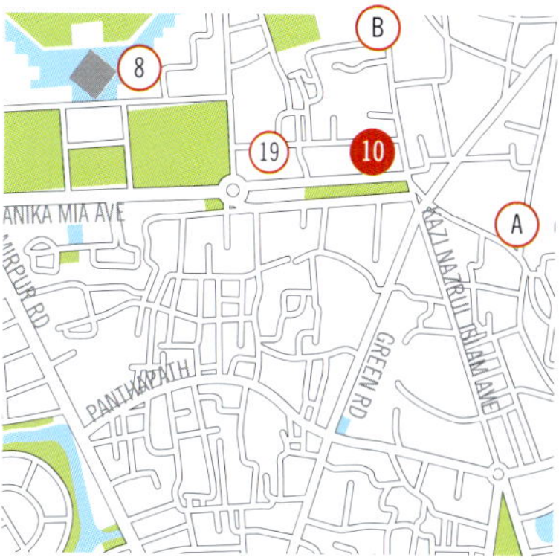

The Bangladesh Agricultural Research Council (BARC) was established in 1973 to coordinate administrative and research activities to modernize agriculture in Bangladesh. In 1978, Shahidullah & Associates Ltd., an architectural and engineering consulting firm, was chosen to design the BARC headquarters on the southeastern edge of Sher-e-Banglanagar. The World Bank provided funding for the project. The BARC site is adjacent to one of Dhaka's busiest intersections, Farmgate, served by the city's arterial north-south Airport Road, in addition to other feeder roads. Architect Rabiul Hussain, of Shahidullah & Associates Ltd., designed a three-story building, clad in red ceramic bricks. Over the years, BARC's headquarters has come to symbolize one of the earliest attempts to find a Bengali "identity" in post-independence Bangladeshi architecture.

While BARC is among several buildings that occupy the L-shaped site, it is the most recognizable from the street and surrounding areas. South of the site are Farmgate and a narrow "road-island" park. Louis Kahn's National Assembly building is nearby, to the west. To the southeast is Holy Cross College. Building height in this area was restricted to four stories when BARC's headquarters was under construction because the site was close to the capital's then-main international airport at Tejgaon.

The 67.97 m (223 ft.) long and 19.2 m (63 ft.) wide rectangular building plan is aligned along the east-west axis, maximizing exposure to the southern breeze and cross ventilation. The three-story building is vertically divided into three functional zones. The first floor features administrative offices; the second floor houses the executive branch. The third floor includes, at the center, a 696.77 sq. m (7,500 sq. ft.) conference room with a seating capacity of 280, flanked by a library and a meeting room, each comprising 125.42 sq. m (1,350 sq. ft.). The total built area of the headquarters is 3,037.93 sq. m (32,700 sq. ft.). The first and second floors are organized along a double-loaded corridor. There are two staircases: One is on the building's east end, and the other is on the west end.

In keeping with the local tradition of projecting roof eaves to protect the building from sun and rain, BARC is essentially two buildings. A brick shell covers the main space. The extra layer moderates the harsh tropical sun and tempers the

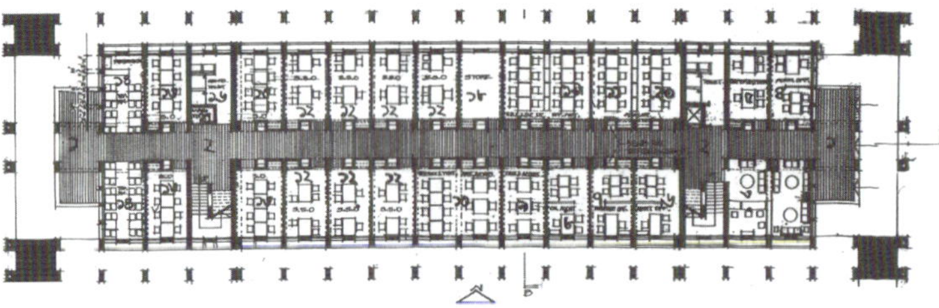

Ground floor plan

driving rain during the monsoon season. This climatic scheme has been a time-tested building practice in the Indian subcontinent. The Mughals have employed this method to ensure thermal comfort and meet the challenges of downpours.

In his National Assembly (Parliament) building, a 15-minute walk from the BARC site, Louis Kahn experimented with a building-within-a-building concept as a climate-mitigating device, eventually producing "transcendental" spatial effects. In planning the Teacher–Student Center (TSC) at the University of Dhaka, the Greek architect-engineer Constantinos Apostolos Doxiadis also has employed different gradations of buildings, providing naturally ventilated and thermally comfortable spaces, a sustainable response to tropical conditions. Architect Muzharul Islam—whose office, Vastukalabid, was a rite of passage since the early 1970s for many young architects, including Rabiul Hussain—also experimented with the critical fusion of climate considerations and modernist aesthetics. The National

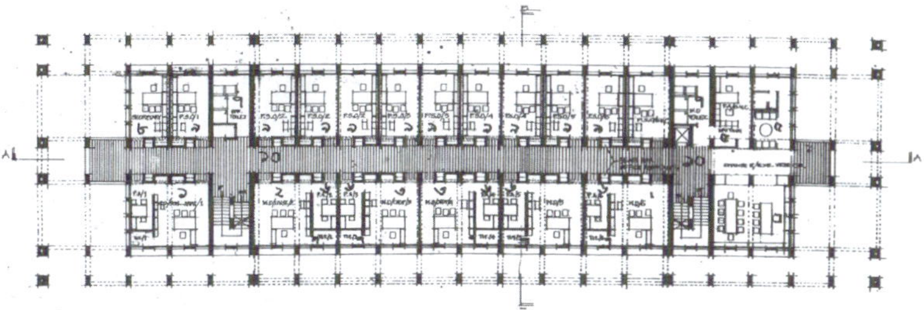

1st floor plan

Institute of Public Administration building (1964–1969), among his other designs, inspired generations of architects to search for the visual language of "critical regionalism" through the lens of climatic aspects.

After the independence of Bangladesh, during the 1970s, the inquiry into a Bengali identity in architecture became a passionate cause, sometimes favoring a tangible visual expression over modernist abstractions. Many Bangladeshi architects came to believe that bricks were the most authentic or organic building material, representing the soil of the riverine country. Since stone is rare, and burnt bricks could be produced abundantly from the indigenous alluvial soil, architects viewed bricks as a phenomenological embodiment of the delta and its culture.

It is difficult to miss the "poetics" of brick in the conceptualization and organization of the BARC headquarters building. Here, one feels the influence of Kahn's magnificent brickwork at the Parliament

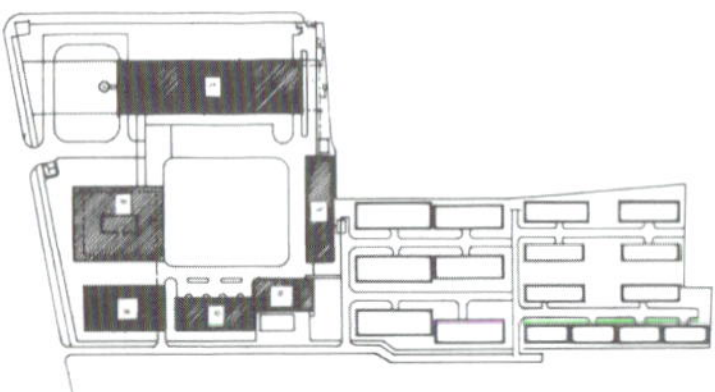

Site plan

Elevation

complex. Echoing the masonry work at that Philadelphia architect's hostels for the Members of the Parliament, architect Rabiul Hussain conceived a brick as the module to lay out his BARC plan. Brick is used as much as possible in exterior and interior walls, columns, beams, floors, ceilings, and stairs. Not only were the basic characteristics of brick reflected in the building, but its volumetric proportions also appear to have been derived from those of a brick. It feels as though the architect has employed a subtractive method to carve out space from one mega-brick! A renowned poet, Rabiul Hussain claims to have been both an architect and a sculptor of this brick building.

At times, the building's "presence" seems more about the exterior than the interior. This is experienced once the visitor enters the headquarters from the covered car portico at the east end. Apart from its linear monotony, the long corridor admits or reflects very little natural light, sometimes requiring artificial illumination during the

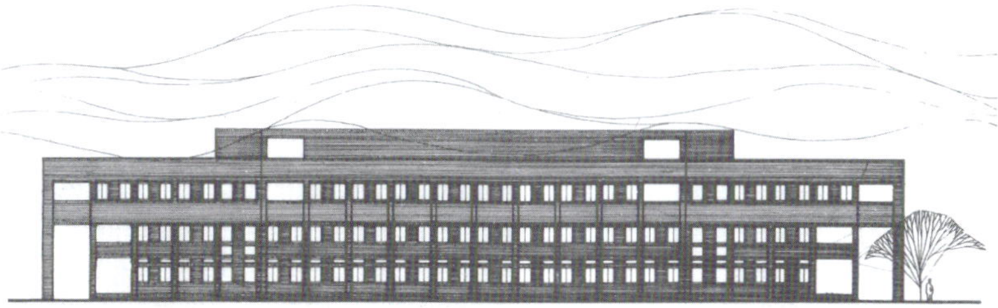

Elevation

day. The chiaroscuro interior conjures up images of a Hindu temple rather than those of an administrative office or a research facility.

Yet the significance of this building is best understood when considered in the historical context of the late 1970s in Bangladesh. It may seem that, at times, the pursuit of an indigenous architectural expression through materiality took precedence over interior organization. A closer look at the BARC headquarters reveals how the edifice negotiated climatic demands of the region with an archetypical and symmetrical spatial modulation. It would not be far-fetched to view the building's plan as a reincarnation of a Buddhist *vihara* (monastery) or a Greek temple like the Parthenon, with its peripteral or single-row colonnade and naos. As a geometrically pure brick structure blending with its verdant base, the regional flavor of the BARC headquarters is unmistakable.

11. NATIONAL MARTYRS' MEMORIAL (JATIYO SMRITI SHOUDHO)

LOCATION: Nabinagar, Dhaka-Aricha Highway (near Nabinagar Bus Stop), Savar 1344
ARCHITECT: Syed Mainul Hossain
CONSTRUCTION SUPERVISOR: Government of Bangladesh Public Works Department
CONSTRUCTION: 1972–1982

PRACTICAL INFORMATION:

Visitors can tour the National Martyrs' Memorial (Jatiyo Smriti Shoudho) from 9 am to 6 pm, 7 days a week. Exceptions: March 22 to 25 and December 12 to 15.

URL: www.visitbangladesh.gov.bd/national-memorial

11 National Martyrs' Memorial (Jatiyo Smriti Shoudho)

NEARBY ATTRACTION:

A Jahangirnagar University (master plan and select buildings; Architect: Muzharul Islam)

Bangladesh's independence after a nine-month liberation war in 1971 was followed by a collective yearning to memorialize the heroism and sacrifice of the *mukti bahini* (freedom fighters). The Bengalis of East Pakistan (now Bangladesh) had long considered that the two wings of Pakistan were governed with asymmetrical priorities, and as a result, the eastern part of the country remained an economic and political backwater. To many observers, the secession of East Pakistan from a unified Pakistan seemed inevitable. When the moment of independence had finally arrived, the need for a powerful symbol to portray its meaning was urgently felt. On December 16, 1982, 11 years after Bangladesh became an independent country, the National Martyrs' Memorial (Jatiyo Smriti Shoudho) was inaugurated. It now stands as a universally admired iconic structure, encapsulating the nation's gratitude toward the men and women who sacrificed their lives for the Bengalis' right to self-rule.

The monument is located at Savar, an industrial suburb about 35.4 km (22 mi.) northwest of Dhaka, the capital city. It rises from a verdant land, somewhat reminiscent of the ruinous mound of the ancient city of Pundranagara at Mahasthangarh, Bogra. The first phase of the project was initiated in 1972, when the government acquired nearly 44.52 ha (110 acres). The supervising agency was the government's Public Works Department. The main complex required 34 ha (84 acres) of land, while the remaining area was allocated for a land-water greenbelt. Access roads were created during the first phase. Mass graves, helipads, parking spaces, and pavements were constructed during the second phase, between 1974 and 1982. Construction of the main monument, greenbelt, and cafeteria occurred in the third phase, in 1982.

A national design competition for the monument took place in 1978. (The previous attempt didn't yield any results.) A 27-year-old architect, Syed Mainul Hossain, won the competition from a pool of 57 participants. As legend has it, Hossain's design was the jury's unanimous choice: It captured most poignantly the new nation's aspiration through an elemental composition of converging planes, achieving a sublime gesture of ascension. Today, the Martyrs' Memorial has become a ubiquitous national symbol.

However, the pyramidal icon at Savar was not conceived as a stand-alone sculptural structure. Rather, the complex was designed

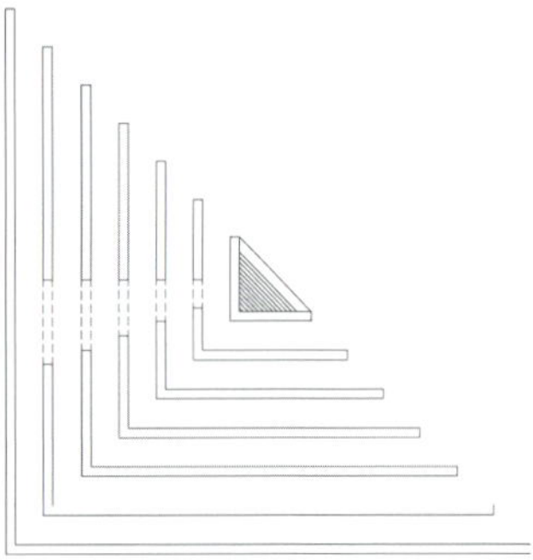

Plan

Site plan

as a holistic landscape, a sort of geometric tapestry weaving together verdant areas, water, walkways, bricks, and and concrete—all culminating with a soaring monument. In many ways, the entire site is a geometric articulation of the deltaic country's physical persona, comprising green areas and water, while the monument is the new nation's ambitious gaze into the future.

From the main northern entrance, the visitor is presented with a strong axial visual connection to the monument. Yet, the journey toward it is deliberately jagged and uneven, unlike, for instance, that of the Taj Mahal, where the approach to the Mughal marble tomb continues along the axis. The tortuous path to the National Martyrs' Memorial symbolizes the nation's difficult path to self-rule, as well as the challenging journey that lies ahead. This winding passage also allows the visitor to see the monument from multiple perspectives, experiencing its dramatically differing configurations and personas, depending on the viewing location. To many, the "magic" of the monument lies in its geometric illusion.

Part of this magic stems from the plan itself. Viewed frontally, the monument appears to be one structure, while in reality, it is an arrangement of seven independent standing concrete plates. Each is an isosceles triangle, but with different dimensions in height and base. The plates are folded in the middle at a 90 degree angle. The highest plate (45.72 m or 150 ft.) has the shortest base (6.1 m or 20 ft.), and the shortest plate has longest base (39.62 m or 130 ft.). The folded plates are placed one after another at a parallel spacing of 2.8 m (9 ft. 2 in.).

The highest plate is at the front, and the shortest is at the back. This configuration creates two powerful parabolic curves that majestically rise toward the sky, when viewed from the front. Yet, to a circumnavigating spectator, the monument presents a singular frozen architectural expression. From the side, the parabolic drama morphs into seven progressively rising triangles. What remains constant is the feeling of ascension.

Numerology plays a crucial role in the monument's composition, recalling the organizing principles of such archetypal structures as the Parthenon, in which numbers were seen as the philosophical foundation of ideal architectural beauty and proportion. The magic number at the National Martyrs' Memorial is 7, which is the number of landmark movements between 1952 and 1971, the period of Bangladesh's nationalist struggle. For instance, among others, the Language Movement in 1952 contains 5+2=7; December 16, the day of independence in 1971, has 1+6=7; and, there were 7 *bir sreshthos* (war heroes) who sacrificed their lives for the cause of liberation.

Even so, the monument's numerical composition seems less important than the overall experience of its captivating geometry. And, ultimately, even this geometry seems less important to the evocation of meditative remembrance that the National Martyrs' Memorial inspires. In 1988, architect Syed Mainul Hossain received the Ekushey Padak Award, one of the country's highest civilian honors, for creating a monument that continues to uplift the spirit of the nation. His other work includes the Bangladesh National Museum at Shahbagh, Dhaka.

12. BANGLADESH CHEMICAL INDUSTRIES CORPORATION (BCIC) HEADQUARTERS

LOCATION: BCIC Bhaban, 30–31 Dilkusha Commercial Area, Motijheel, Dhaka 1000
ARCHITECT: Bashirul Haq
CONSULTANT: Bashirul Haq & Associates Ltd.
CONSTRUCTION: 1981–1987

PRACTICAL INFORMATION:

Visitors to the Bangladesh Chemical Industries Corporation (BCIC) headquarters should submit a request 3 days in advance. Premises are open from 9 am to 1 pm and from 2 pm to 5 pm, Sunday to Thursday.

Contact:
Mr. Mohammad Abdul Jalil Khan
General Menager (Civil)
Estate Management Department, BCIC
Dhaka 1000

Phone: +88-02-9559281

E-Mail: emd.gm@bcic.gov.bd

2 Armenian Church of the Holy Resurrection
3 Ahsan Manzil
4 Curzon Hall
6 Teacher–Student Center (TSC)
7 Kamalapur Railway Station
12 Bangladesh Chemical Industries Corporation (BCIC) Headquarters
18 Museum of Independence and Independence Monument

NEARBY ATTRACTIONS:

A Bangabhaban (The President's Residence)
B Bangabandhu National Stadium

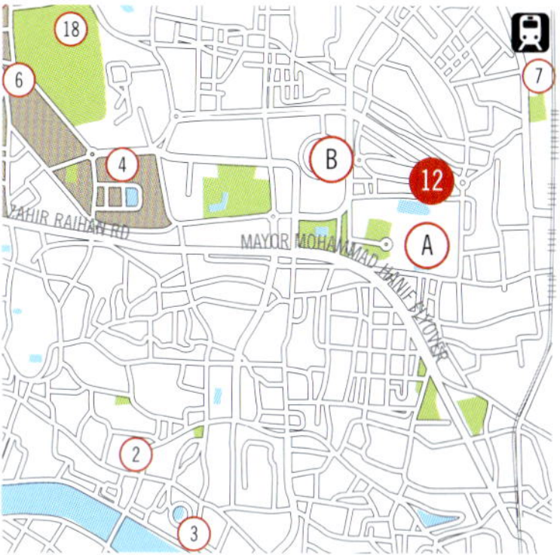

With Bangladesh's emergence as an independent country in 1971, Dhaka became the capital city. For the new nation, the decade of the 1970s was a complex tapestry of optimism and pessimism. The euphoria of liberation soon dissipated within the maze of political unrest, assassinations, and military interventions. Reminiscent of many other post-independence countries in social turmoil, a contested search for a national identity ensued. Furthermore, the Cold War-era politics—particularly, the shifting fault lines along the relationships among the United States, the Soviet Union, China, and India—complicated the internal affairs of Bangladesh.

Amidst the social tension of the 1970s, a new generation of ambitious architects burst forth onto the architectural scene of Bangladesh. The outcomes of a few national architectural competitions revealed new visions of modernity, building technology, and architectural space. Institutional and commercial buildings were no longer bland boxes, comprising corridors and rooms.

Bashirul Haq is a pioneering architect, who, in many ways, epitomized the modernist impulses in Bangladeshi architecture during the decades of the 1970s and 1980s. In 1977, he won the national design competition for the Bangladesh Chemical Industries Corporation (BCIC) headquarters in downtown Dhaka's Dilkusha Commercial Area. His entry showcased a new type of design energy that synthesized modernist aesthetics with a reasoned consideration for the local climate, a low budget, and an urban context.

One of the largest sector corporations in Bangladesh at the time, BCIC needed to consolidate its six scattered directorates and a large number of rental offices for general managers, managers, and supporting personnel into one headquarters building, to run the corporation more efficiently. For this purpose, a 0.25 ha (0.61 acre) parcel of land was acquired in Dilkusha. Bashirul Haq's winning proposal was trendsetting from a host of urban, architectural, and building-technology viewpoints.

Haq fully exploited the site's location between two parallel urban thoroughfares, to provide access from both north and south, integrating the BCIC headquarters into its intense urban environment. His 20-story building is set back considerably from the road.

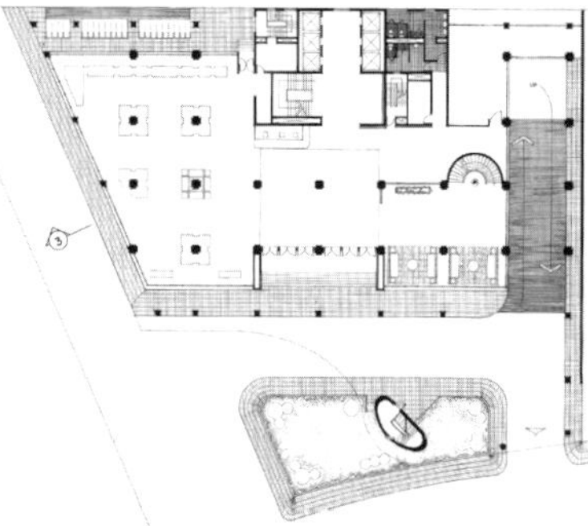

Ground floor plan

4th floor plan

A bold proposition in a land-scarce downtown area, the exposed-concrete edifice allowed the gritty urbanscape around it to enter the site, blurring the boundary between public and private. Volumetrically, the building's composition is simple. It consists of a tower slab and a protruding, low-rise building mass, creating a dynamic tension between the regularity of the office space in the tower and the obliquely organized auditorium that juts out from the second floor, with a fluid horizontal sweep. The "floating" auditorium provides a covered vehicular porch, a welcome convenience during the monsoon season.

Another novel idea was a small, undulating garden that serves two purposes: It creates a pleasant and subtle barrier between the busy thoroughfare and the building's site. And, it democratizes its environment by rendering unnecessary the need for a protective wall. The garden presents less of an urban oasis than a small pocket of green, marked by tropical plants and pebbles, recalling the

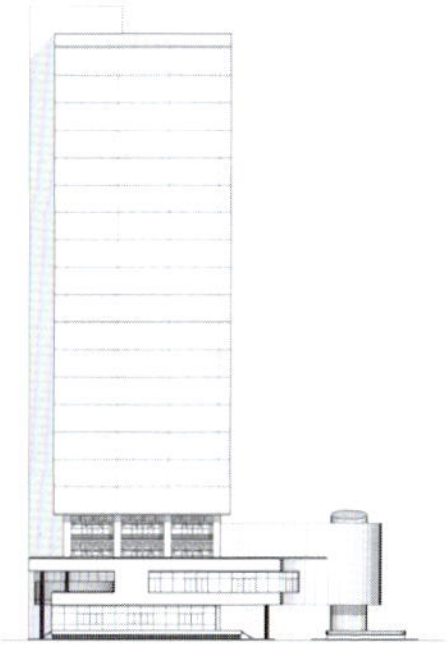

Left side elevation

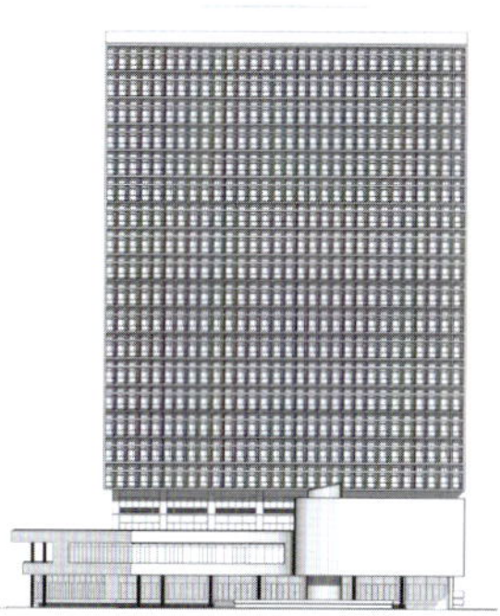

Front elevation

simplicity and organic qualities of a Japanese garden. The solid concrete shaft that rises from the garden supports the auditorium above, while providing an exit stairway from it.

BCIC's headquarters comprises a total floor area of 28,103.17 sq. m (302,500 sq. ft.). The ground floor contains two spacious, double-story lobbies. One is for the general entrance; the other, with an adjacent semicircular stairway, provides access to the auditorium on the second floor. The ground floor also includes a reception area, office space, the security office, rental space, an electric substation, and the elevator/stairway shaft. Each of the six elevators has a carrying capacity of 13 passengers.

In addition to the two-story auditorium and backstage, the second floor has a circular mosque, rental space, and refreshment areas. The third floor incorporates a library, office spaces, and the auditorium, as well as a cafeteria that can accommodate 90 patrons. This cafeteria extends onto a large outdoor terrace that could be

used for gatherings or functions in pleasant weather.

The tower slab rises from the fourth floor, which houses executive office, board, and conference rooms, as well as basic office areas. Every typical floor has common areas and a tea room. The basement accommodates parking for 37 cars, car services, an underground water reservoir and pump house, a standby generator, storage facilities for maintenance, and a driver waiting area, among other features.

The BCIC headquarters introduces a few structural novelties to Bangladesh. This is the country's first high-rise building with a flat-plate system and precast concrete fins that serve as a brise-soleil (shades or screens to temper the sun's direct light and heat). The waffle slab at the entrance creates a visual experience that was unique to the local architectural scene. And, the overall quality of concrete craftsmanship in the building is also extraordinary. The fact that there was no native typology for high-rise buildings made it particularly challenging. Yet, Bashirul Haq saw this as an opportunity for both innovation and experimentation.

Haq was born in 1938 in Brahmanbaria in the northeast section of Dhaka. He received his Bachelor of Architecture degree from the National College of Arts, in Lahore, Pakistan, in 1964. (This was the same year that construction of Louis Kahn's National Assembly building began, in Dhaka.) Before he left for the United States in 1971, to pursue higher education in architecture, Haq worked in the offices of Bangladesh's first modernist architect Muzharul Islam. He was also affiliated with T. Abdul Hussain Thariani, designer of the country's national mosque, Baitul Mukarram, in downtown Dhaka. Haq received his Master of Architecture degree from the University of New Mexico, in 1975. Afterward, he joined the architectural firm Kallmann, McKinnell & Wood (KMW), in Boston. Incidentally, one of Haq's KMW projects included a master plan for his alma mater, in New Mexico.

Bashirul Haq was fortunate to find a mentor in Fazlur Rahman Khan (popularly known as F. R. Khan). A fellow countryman, Khan was a partner of the famed Chicago-based architectural/engineering firm Skidmore, Owings & Merrill (SOM) and structural designer of Chicago's Sears

Tower (renamed Willis Tower), the tallest building in the world from 1973 to 1998. The SOM stalwart took Haq under his wing and encouraged him to join his Chicago firm as an architect.

However, as fate would have it, Bashirul Haq, already in his late 30s, chose to return home, to Bangladesh. In 1977, he established Bashirul Haq & Associates. Remarkably, Haq won the design competition for BCIC that same year. In the early 1980s, F. R. Khan visited Bashirul Haq's office and advised him to rotate the BCIC building's orthogonal waffle slab at the ground level by 45 degrees for more structural durability!

Thanks to his architectural education in America during the heyday of High Modernism, prior to the onslaught of Postmodernism, Bashirul Haq absorbed the influence of many Western masters, particularly Le Corbusier. The BCIC tower in Dilkusha recalls the sublime simplicity of Lucio Costa and Oscar Niemeyer's Ministry of Education and Health (1937–1943) in Rio de Janeiro. Le Corbusier's style also inspired those architects. Arguably the first modernist building of the Americas, the Ministry of Education and Health introduced a building typology that had sustained appeal across the world.

Like the 14-story modernist icon in Rio de Janeiro, the BCIC headquarters presents the geometrical composition of a vertical block (although with an oblique side) and a horizontal form. The allure of both buildings hinges on the dynamic confrontation of a soaring rectangular slab and a free-form, "floating" lower level that acts as a public entrance "canopy." The United Nations headquarters building in New York City (1952) and Brasilia's National Congress building (1960) present similar formal arrangements.

Bashirul Haq, however, co-opts this modernist typology for a particular urban context in Dhaka, with perceptive adaptations to climatic conditions. The tower block's longer axis is more or less along the east-west axis, maximizing the north-south cross ventilation and natural light for the office spaces. And, the glazing is set back within a rhythmic composition of vertical and horizontal louvers. (The BCIC headquarters is partially air-conditioned. Today, however, the crass placement of individual office air-conditioners somewhat diminishes the glazing's original beauty.) Popular with the building's users, most of the offices in the tower block feature natural ventilation, in addition to invigorating aerial views of the city.

Today, visitors to the building encounter makeshift street bazaars—offering vegetables, spices, and household merchandise—adjacent to the BCIC headquarters. The fact that the building could generate a micro-urban environment around it is, perhaps, a testament to its landmark status. Most of all, visiting the BCIC headquarters, one gets a fascinating glimpse into the evolution of modernist architecture in Bangladesh and into Dhaka as a bustling city.

13. SINGLE-FAMILY HOUSE

13A
KAMALUDDIN RESIDENCE
LOCATION: House 43/A, Road 6-A, Dhanmondi Residential Area, Dhaka 1209
ARCHITECT: Shamsul Wares
CONSTRUCTION: 1984–1987

13B
S. A. RESIDENCE
LOCATION: House 37, Road 100, Gulshan 2, Dhaka 1212
ARCHITECT: Rafiq Azam
CONSTRUCTION: 2005–2010

13C
KARIM RESIDENCE
LOCATION: House 375, Road 9-B, Block D, Bashundhara Residential Area, Dhaka 1229
ARCHITECT: Salauddin Ahmed Patash
CONSTRUCTION: 2006–2010

PRACTICAL INFORMATION:

These are private properties and, therefore, not open to the public. Visitors might receive special permission by contacting each architect.

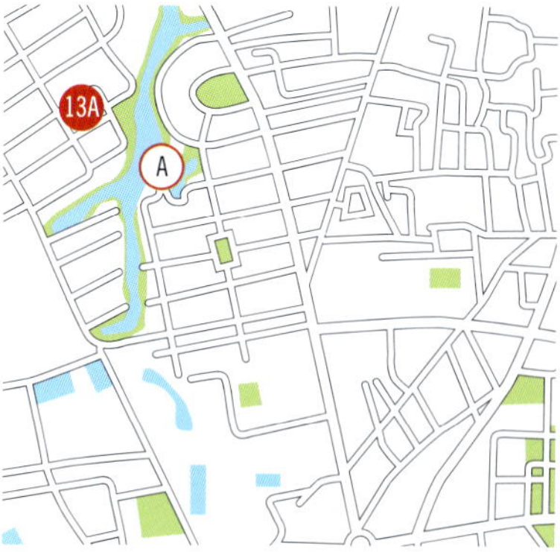

13A Kamaluddin Residence
13B S. A. Residence
13C Karim Residence
16 Grameenphone Corporate Headquarters (GP House)
20 Akash Prodip Apartment Building

NEARBY ATTRACTION:

A Dhanmondi Lake

Dhaka's planned neighborhoods, such as Dhanmondi, Gulshan, and Banani, historically featured an urban legacy of single-family houses. Before the capital city started to grow rapidly from the 1980s onward, the urban middle class typically preferred one- or two-story single-family houses, placed on a plot of green, perhaps a synthesis of urban living and pastoral memory. However, as Bangladesh's urban population rose from 7 percent during the time of independence in 1971 to more than 20 percent during the early 1990s (primarily as a result of rural-to-urban migration), and the demand for urban housing was manifold, single-family houses seemed increasingly untenable as a socially and commercially viable housing option.

During this transitional period, profit-motivated real estate developers emerged as powerful economic actors, playing a key role in replacing single-family houses with multistory apartment complexes. A casual walk today through Dhanmondi, Gulshan, Kalabagan, Muhammadpur, and Uttara, among other areas, reveals how Bangladesh's urban landscape has changed dramatically during the past two decades or so, from low-lying towns to "high-rise" metropolises.

Yet, despite Dhaka's growing reputation as one of the most densely populated cities in the world, wealthy urbanites continued to commission architects to build sumptuous single-family houses as a sign of their social status and economic prosperity. A burgeoning class of urban entrepreneurs—who made their fortunes in the country's export-oriented ready-made garments industry, manufacturing and transportation sectors, construction industry, and consumer market—emulated "old money" and emerged as a new generation of architectural patrons, investing hefty amounts of money to build their signature single-family houses.

This section highlights three such commissions.

Kamaluddin Residence

In the mid-1980s, architect and renowned educator Shamsul Wares —who starred in Nathaniel Kahn's acclaimed documentary, *My Architect: A Son's Journey* (2003)—designed Kamaluddin Residence, a three story single-family house, situated on a corner plot of roughly 278.71 sq. m (3,000 sq. ft.), in Dhanmondi. A veteran journalist who worked for the Hong Kong-based *Far Eastern Economic Review*, Kamaluddin wanted a house that would provide his family with some privacy and an opportunity for independent living in a growing city.

An unflinching modernist and a firm believer in the universality of a modern language in architecture, Wares designed a compact house, characterized by bold inclined roofs and white plastered walls. Guided by the principle that a geometrically abstract building would not only fit into the urban context of Dhaka, but also enhance it with a modern aesthetic, the architect played an important pedagogical role in Bangladeshi architecture, downplaying the hackneyed dichotomy of modernity and tradition. This, however, does not mean that his building ignored its specific urban context.

In fact, Kamaluddin Residence ingenuously transforms the tight plot into an architectural experience of spacious interiority, facilitated by a mobility of space in section. The inclined roofs, 45 degrees in one direction and 60 degrees in another, enable a cascading flow of space from the top, establishing a continuous floor-to-floor relationship. The house's combination of gleaming white walls, mustard-colored tiles, and sensible distribution of solids and voids conjures up an amalgamated image of Le Corbusier's white, boxy building and the sparkling traditional edifices of Santorini, a Greek island in the Aegean Sea.

Elevation

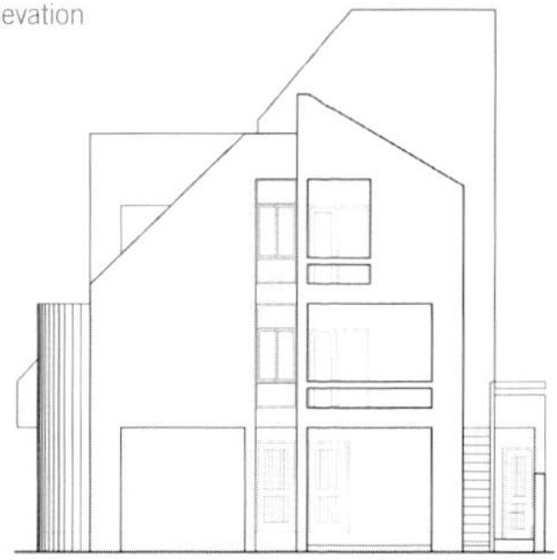

Elevation

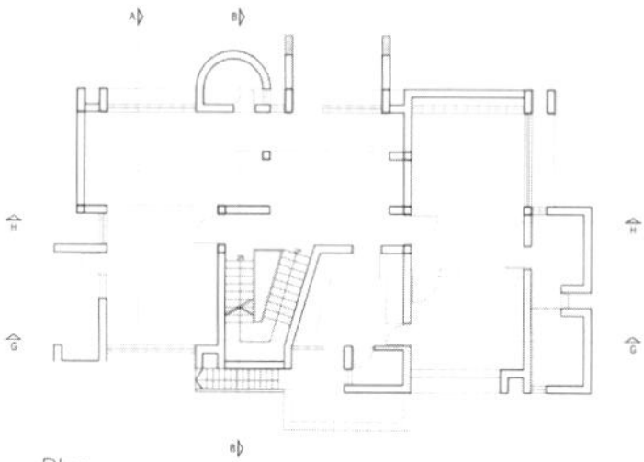

Plan

The influence of Richard Meier's early designs and, more broadly, the collective work of New York's Five Architects (Peter Eisenman, Michael Graves, Charles Gwathmey, John Hejduk, and Richard Meier), who banded together in 1972 to publish and market their high-end residential houses, is palpable in Kamaluddin Residence. The kind of aesthetic purity and formal experimentation that the Five Architects celebrated in their work resonated with architects around the world, who saw no essential conflict between universal modernity and particularities of social conditions. Wares showcased this architectural attitude in Kamaluddin Residence by utilizing a sharp sense of proportionality, sculptural simplicity, and formal unity. In many ways, this building could be viewed as an emblematic representation of single-family houses built during the 1980s in Dhaka.

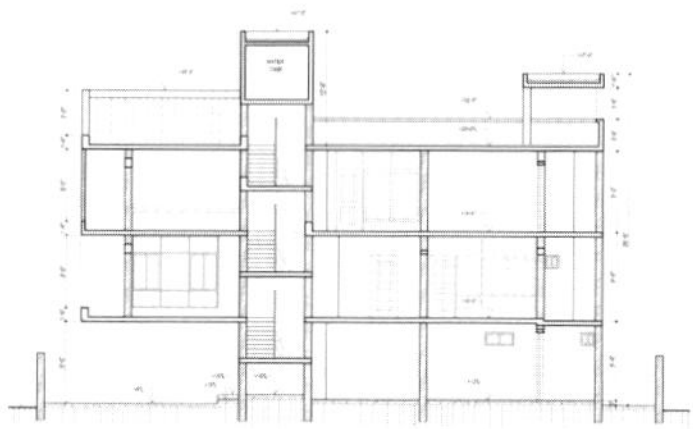

Section

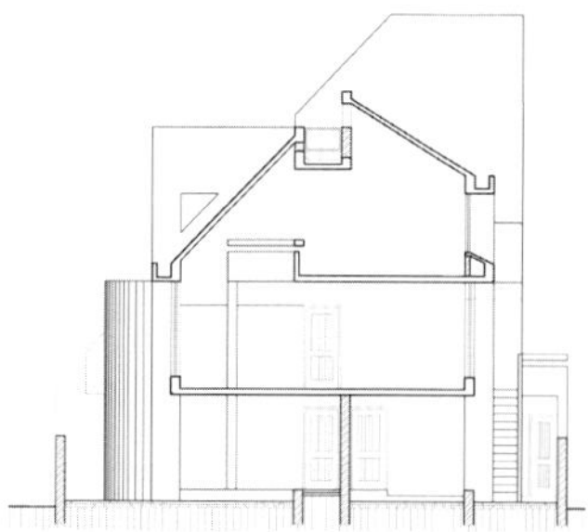

Section

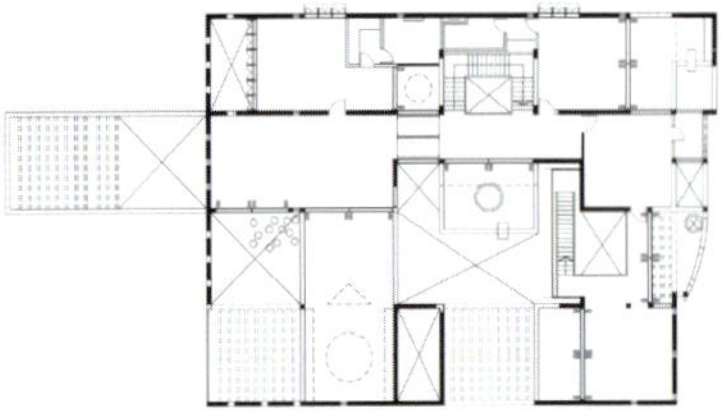

1st floor plan

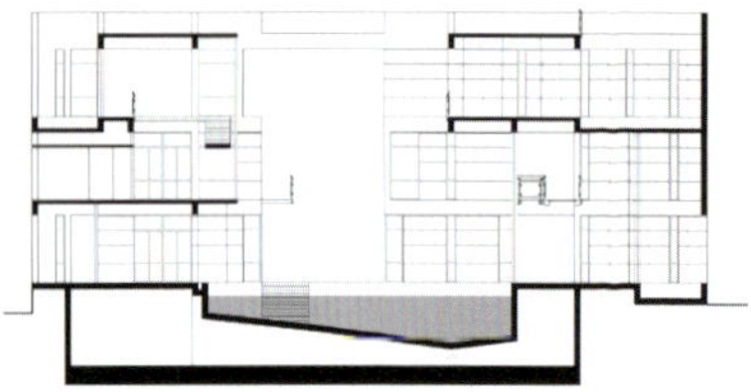

Section

S. A. Residence

Architect Rafiq Azam's S. A. Residence in the city's upscale Gulshan area presents a prime example of how the moneyed class in Bangladesh envisioned the single-family house in the early 21st century. This nearly US$2 million house, comprising a floor area of more than 1,858.06 sq. m (20,000 sq. ft.), creates a multilayered interior world of affluence, luxury, and serenity in the midst of a chaotic, bustling city. It also elevates the social standing of its owner during Bangladesh's own "gilded" age, taking shape from the late 20th century onward.

To understand the social significance of S. A. Residence requires a familiarity with Bangladesh's economic growth since the early 1990s. Its GDP has been rising at a respectable 5 percent or more a year. One of the main drivers of Bangladesh's economic success has been large-scale, export-oriented industrialization, which, in turn, benefits various public and private

sectors. According to the London-based think tank Legatum Institute, Bangladesh's "prosperity index" (in 2013)—based on multiple variables about economic performance, entrepreneurship, governance, health, and education—revealed remarkable advancements in the social and economic indicators.

This prosperity also had a major transformative effect on the country's architectural landscape. The willingness of the affluent class to make a status-conscious statement through the design of their residence dovetailed with the fledgling industry of professional architectural practice across the country. Many architects saw this mutually beneficial relationship as a timely opportunity to search for an architecture of substance and deeper meaning.

Rafiq Azam is one of them. He graduated from the architecture program at the Bangladesh University of Engineering and Technology (BUET), Dhaka, in the late 1980s. Currently, Azam is the principal architect of Shatotto, a Dhaka-based architectural firm that focuses on what it calls "green living." His client, Salauddin Ahmed, who has a courier-service business in Bangladesh, desired a house that would recall his childhood, spent in and inspired by the tranquil setting of rural Bangladesh. As an urban entrepreneur, Ahmed knew that he could never return permanently to his ancestral village. However, he yearned to make tangible part of his childhood memory in the midst of a frenzied city of 18 million.

Azam faced two key challenges. First, the architect needed to translate his client's vision by delving deep into the mythology of Bengali vernacular—as expressed through this deltaic land's riverine geography, landscape, canals and boats, and mystical music. And, second, Azam wanted to transcend the familiar visuality of the Bengali village—typically marked by its pastoral homestead wrapping around ponds and courtyards—to achieve something meditatively modern, yet invested in Bengal's *genius loci,* or spirit of place.

At the entry level, S. A. Residence is organized around a central pond-courtyard, which is also a swimming pool. In addition to providing living, dining, sleeping, and utility spaces at the ground level, there is a conscious attempt to create a performative environment of quiet, light, rain, green, and fluid space—all choreographed on a stage set of concrete and wood.

The second floor presents an almost Kafkaesque return to the Bengali wilderness, including such spaces as "crop field," "rain room," and "bamboo bush." The third floor contains bedrooms of various sizes, while space flows both horizontally and vertically throughout the entire building. All in all, this is luxury at its absurd heights, yet the architect was able to express it with dignified, restrained, and introspective felicity.

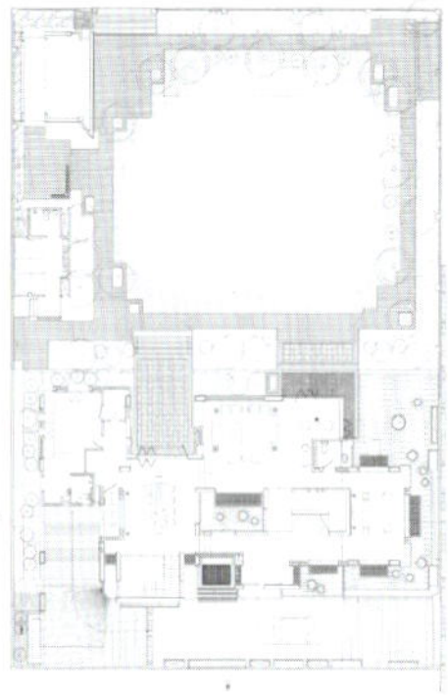

Ground floor plan

Karim Residence

Architect Salauddin Ahmed Patash's Karim Residence in Bashundhara Residential Area, in northeast Dhaka, is another example of a high-end single-family house that creates an interior realm of bliss and comfort, as well as a prestigious urban address. Patash was trained in architecture in the United States, first at Portland State University, Oregon, and then at the University of Pennsylvania, Philadelphia. After working for several years in the United States, he returned home and began to practice a different kind of architecture: a cultural synthesis in which East and West became lived experiences, rather than abstract categories. Karim Residence sits on an expansive plot (1,300.64 sq. m or 14,000 sq. ft.), a rare occurrence in a hyper-congested metropolis. The house occupies about 45 percent of the plot, while the rest is lush green. The concrete parasol roofs that jut out boldly from the building mass are

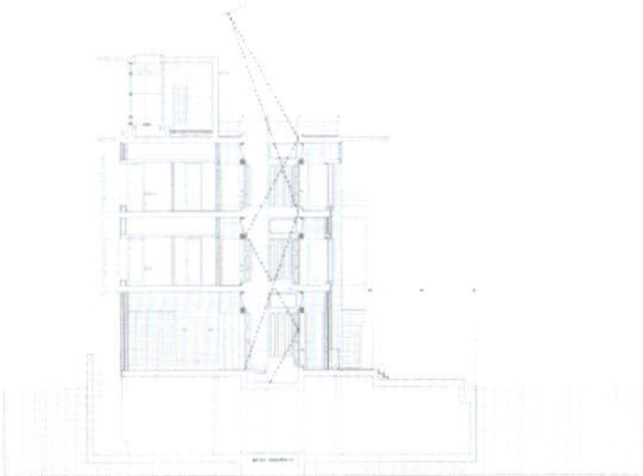

Section

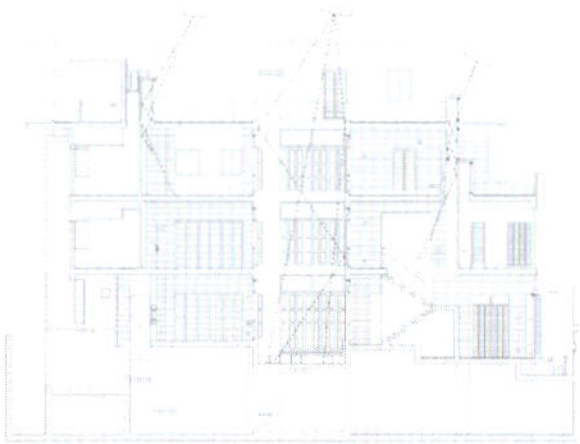

Section

subtle reminders of the need to negotiate the driving tropical rain—clearly, a modern allusion to a Bengali hut's canopy. A quartet of design considerations seems to drive the imagination of the house: materiality, water, light, and the indoor/outdoor relationship. A symphonious combination of red brick and concrete on the outside serves as a prologue to an interior drama. The protagonists of this drama are water, light, and space, all performing an omnidirectional dance.

The result is a richly tactile and kinetic interior that refuses to be interior at all, as light, pulled-out verandahs, and permeability together whisper a fluid spatial story. While interior morphs into exterior and vice versa, the architecture provides a therapeutic experience of both nature and its built analog. It is a rich man's house—costing US$1.3 million—but it does not flaunt nouveau riche luxury.

14. PRIYO PRANGAN APARTMENT COMPLEX

LOCATION: 2 Paribagh, Dhaka 1000
ARCHITECT: Uttam Kumar Saha
CONSTRUCTION: 1989–1991
AWARD: Institute of Architects Bangladesh Multifamily Residential Building Design Award, 2000.

PRACTICAL INFORMATION:

The Priyo Prangan apartment complex is a private property and, therefore, not open to the public. Visitors might receive special permission by contacting the architect.

5 Faculty of Fine Arts
6 Teacher–Student Center (TSC)
14 Priyo Prangan Apartment Complex
18 Museum of Independence and Independence Monument.

NEARBY ATTRACTIONS:

A Ramna Park
B Bangladesh National Museum
C Bishwo Shahitto Kendro (World Literature Center; Architects: Mahmudul Anwar Riyaad and Mamnoon Murshed Chowdhury)

Priyo Prangan, a multistory, multifamily residential complex designed by architect Uttam Kumar Saha, is considered a pioneering project in the private sector of real estate development in Bangladesh. This housing estate at Paribagh, located within the center of Dhaka, signaled the advent of a new building typology that began to dominate the cityscape of the capital from the early 1990s. It was a flagship building of Priyo Prangan Housing Ltd. (later renamed Hamid Real Estate Construction Ltd.), representing a growing economic sector in the country. (This sector contributed 8.63 percent to the GDP in 2001–2002.) Comprising such iconic features as a terraced roofline, exposed concrete, roof gardens, colorful railings, and spacious community areas, Priyo Prangan has inspired subsequent real estate development in Dhaka and beyond.

In the wake of the country's independence in 1971, Bangladesh, historically an agrarian country, began to urbanize rapidly. The country's total urban population rose from 7 percent in 1971 to 31.1 percent in 2010. Impoverished rural migrants began to flock to major cities, particularly the capital, Dhaka, in search of employment and better lives. It was not long before Dhaka became a megacity: Its population skyrocketed from 1.8 million in 1974 to more than 6 million in 1991 and to 18 million in 2015. The capital city's massive population boom created an unsustainable demand on urban land, and in return, land values increased. (In the city's Gulshan area, land costs were $11,000 per sq. m in 2012, more or less the same as in Manhattan, New York.)

Public-sector housing failed to meet the demand, and in this vacuum, private real estate companies flourished rapidly. For instance, in the early 1980s, there were only 5 real estate companies in the country. By 1988, the number had increased to 42. As private developers became key actors in the city's housing market, a trade association was needed to regulate the real estate sector and to ensure fair competition among its members. The Real Estate and Housing Association of Bangladesh was formed in 1991, with 11 members. By 2009, membership had reached 589. The stratospheric rise of private real estate developers suggested that there was a robust market for high-density, multifamily apartments, even though affordability remained a major hurdle.

Before the growth of multifamily apartment buildings, the urban middle class preferred individual plot-based single-family houses. However, many factors made owner-built houses untenable: rapidly rising land values, scarcity of buildable land in Dhaka, challenges of construction, and a corrupt bureaucracy that often made securing permission to build a prohibitive process. Consequently, for the urban middle class, buying ready-made apartments was the most viable option. It also avoided the lengthy and worrisome construction process.

The real estate business promised to be profitable for all three key stakeholders: the landowner, the developer, and the prospective apartment buyer. The landowner sells the land to the developer for a profit and a mutually agreed upon share of apartments. The developer typically incurs a bank loan to build the apartment complex and sells the apartments to buyers, either before or after construction. The developer makes a profit and the buyer owns a piece of property, popularly deemed a prudent investment.

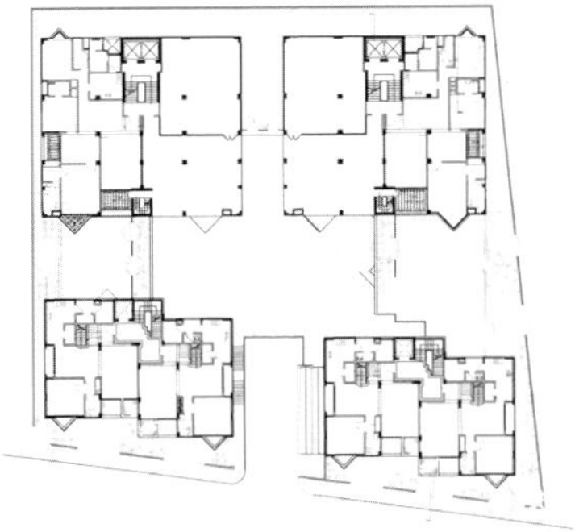

Ground floor plan

6th floor plan

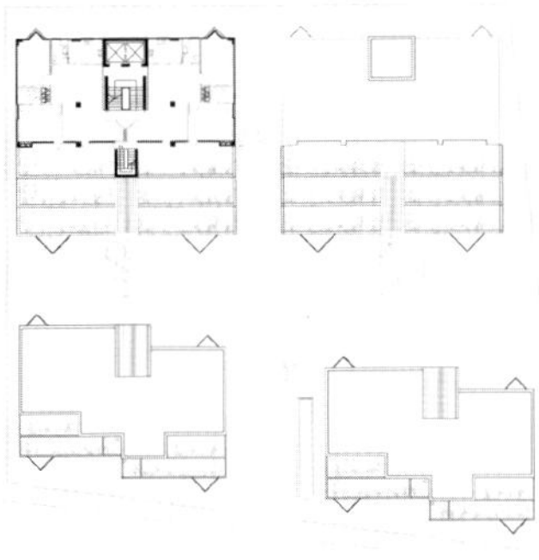

15th floor plan

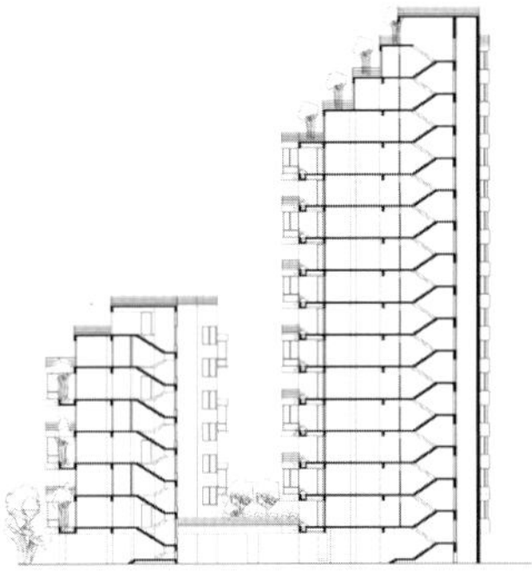

Section

Despite the high costs of apartments, buyers were motivated by a number of factors: A gated community of families provides a sense of security; apartment buildings include spaces for community activities, play areas for children, a prayer room, and a roof garden; there are secure parking facilities; and there is cooperative management of the building. Thus, in the early 1990s, a presumed win-win situation for all stakeholders rapidly created a thriving real estate industry in Dhaka and the rest of the country.

Architect Uttam Kumar Saha's Priyo Prangan became the first-generation face of this industry. Saha received his Bachelor of Architecture degree from the Bangladesh University of Engineering and Technology (BUET), in 1981. Inspired by the contemplative modernism of architects Muzharul Islam and Alvar Aalto and by Chetana, the local architectural study group, Saha represented a new generation of architects who emerged during the 1980s with a view toward creating a "critical regionalism" in Bangladeshi architecture. His first built

project, Bisha Shahitya Kendro, means "a center for world literature." (Unfortunately, it was demolished recently.) Saha focused on the concept of a simple pastoral courtyard, found in a typical Bengali rural homestead, and he incorporated local building materials and construction techniques.

The idea for Bisha Shahitya Kendro was furthered at Priyo Prangan, a multifamily residential estate comprising 56 apartments in two south-facing towers, with each tower featuring dual heights. The southern roadside buildings are 8 stories, and the rear buildings are 17 stories. Both towers are connected at the second floor by an open-air children's play area, which also serves as the community hub for the entire complex. In fact, the name of the complex, derives from this community courtyard; *priyo* means "dear," and *prangan* means "open field."

To maximize profit, developers are generally interested in stacking as many

identical units as possible, often creating a monotonous box. However, because of the relative scarcity of a model for this building typology, Saha could introduce variety into the building program by designing two different types of unit plans: a 192.77 sq. m (2,075 sq. ft.) single unit and a 241.55 sq. m (2,600 sq. ft.) duplex.

Priyo Prangan also features cost-saving innovations. In the 17-story towers, the staircase, along with fire-escape access, serves two identical units per floor, flanking the service core. However, lift access is provided in between two floors, stopping at the landing level, thereby reducing costs. And, because high-rise living was still not part of the cultural imagination in the country, Saha sought to reshape the experience of traditional ground level living by incorporating kitchen gardens and planters. Typical units include three or four bedrooms, formal living and dining areas, a family room, a kitchen, a maid's room, and storage. The service core and kitchen areas are located on the north side, maximizing the southern exposure for bedrooms and living areas.

To take advantage of the road frontage—which is only 12.2 m (40 ft.) wide—Saha introduced broad, terraced roofs. Because the building code at that time required that every story above the ninth floor be recessed by 3.05 m (10 ft.) per floor, Saha terraced the top six floors in the taller buildings and the top two floors of the shorter buildings. This was a novelty for Dhaka's skyline. In addition, small projecting triangular verandahs give the building a unique urban profile.

Access to the site is from the south, and the south-facing orientation of the entire complex helps keep it naturally ventilated. The east and west façades have minimum fenestration to reduce heat gain. Most likely considered too expensive, the complex has no basement parking.

Priyo Prangan still retains part of its original trendsetting persona. Its contrasting juxtaposition of exposed concrete and orange-hued railings, along with its progressively recessed roofline and triangular mini verandahs, conjures up a memorable urban image. Gently rising from a base of leafy trees, it continues to pique people's interest. In 2000, Priyo Prangan received the Institute of Architects Bangladesh Design Award in the Multifamily Residential Building category.

15. SCHOLASTICA SCHOOL

LOCATION: Plot 2, Roads 8 & 9, Sector 1, Uttara Model Town, Dhaka 1230
ARCHITECT: Jalal Ahmed
ASSOCIATE ARCHITECTS: Kayesh Tanim and Mumtaz Anwar
CONSTRUCTION: 1997–2000

PRACTICAL INFORMATION:

Scholastica School is a private property and, therefore, not open to the public. Visitors should contact the school to arrange a tour. The school's authorities reserve all rights of access to the campus.

Contact:
Syeda Madiha Murshed
Director of Scholastica (Pvt.) Ltd.

Phone:
+88-02-58952753 or +88-02-7913663 or +88-02-58950488 or +88-02-58959544 or +88-02-58956053

E-Mail: madiha_murshed@ascent-bd.com or managing_director@scholasticabd.com or madiha_murshed@scholasticabd.com

15 Scholastica School
17 BRAC–Aarong Commercial Center

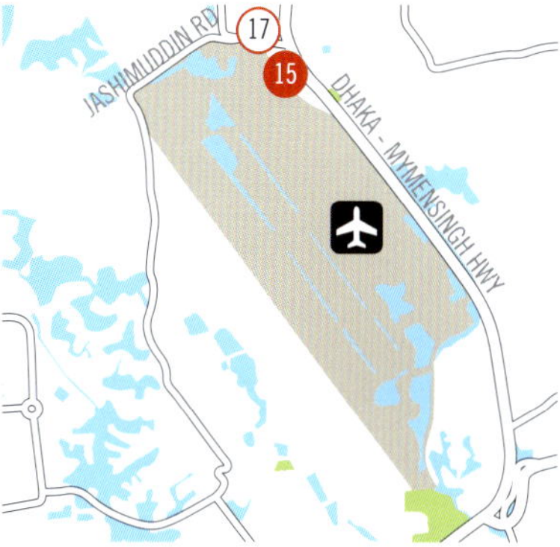

The growth of privately funded English-language schools has been an important urban phenomenon in Bangladesh since the 1980s. During the 1970s, in the wake of independence, when the nationalist pitch was high, the government mandated that the native language Bangla be used as the sole mode for education. Government funding generally went to Bengali-language private-sector schools.

However, the rising middle class viewed learning English as an essential tool for social mobility and prestige, and the demand for English-language schools began to surge during the 1980s. Because there had been no sustained government patronage of such schools, they operated in scattered rental spaces or multistory residential buildings across the city. These adaptive facilities typically relied on very limited space and had no allocation for recreational areas, for such activities as outdoor games. Generally located in dense residential areas (Dhanmondi, for instance), they contributed to the city's already worsening traffic congestion, particularly during daily rush hours.

The status of English-language schools began to change in the 1990s. As tuition revenues for these schools increased, their owners and trustee boards exerted greater influence on government policymakers. These private school executives sought to move their facilities to designed school campuses. Their aim was twofold: to provide students of all grades with access to a comprehensive education under one roof and to create a learning environment that would foster all-around development. A new urban building typology began to take shape.

One of the first English-language schools to herald this new urban typology was Scholastica School in Uttara Model Town, a planned satellite neighborhood north of Dhaka's international airport. (Two other schools that later had designed their own campuses were International School Dhaka and Hermann Gmeiner School of SOS Children's Villages International.) Scholastica was established, in 1977, under the leadership of Yasmeen Murshed, "to build curious, knowledgeable, and caring young individuals, who will be equipped to tackle head-on the challenges of our modern-day 'global village.'"

Given the school's large student population, it now has campuses in several locations, including Uttara, Dhanmondi, Mirpur, and Gulshan. Scholastica's Sector 1 Uttara

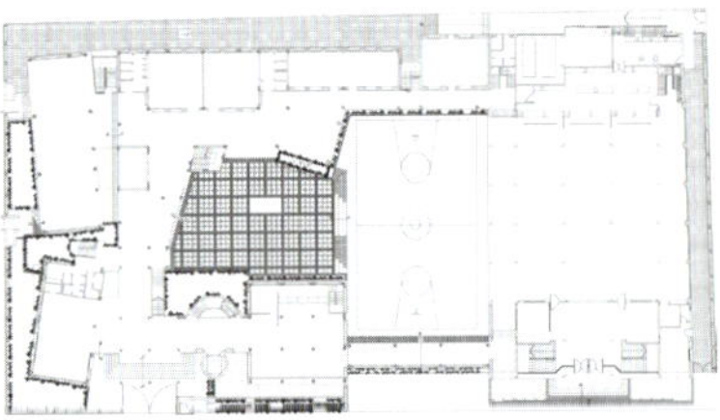

Ground floor plan

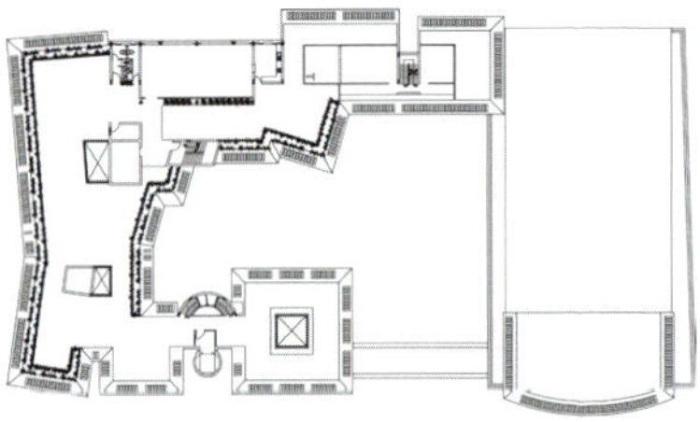

Roof plan

school, situated on 0.45 ha (1.10 acres), has a total built area of 12,077.4 sq. m (130,000 sq. ft.), with a construction cost of US$2.5 million. The plot was purchased from the Government of Bangladesh Capital Development Authority (RAJUK). Originally, this Uttara site had been earmarked for educational institutions. Longitudinally parallel to Mirpur Road, the city's main north-south thoroughfare, the land is bounded by roads on three sides, with a private medical college on the west. The tight plot in a dense urban area called for a tall building to house the senior division of the school community, comprising 1,200 students and more than 150 teachers.

In 1997, Scholastica chose architect Jalal Ahmed, of J. A. Architects, to undertake this challenging project. Ahmed had received his Architecture degree from the Bangladesh University of Engineering and Technology (BUET), in 1983. Since that time, he has been in private practice and

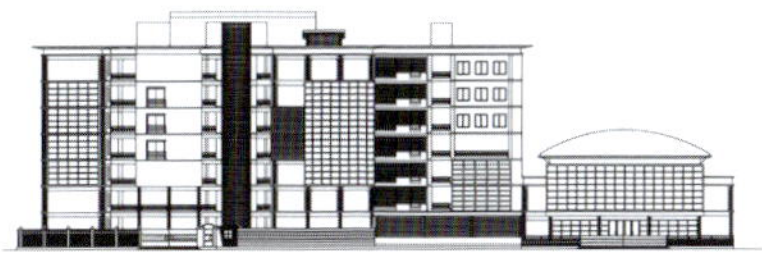

Elevation

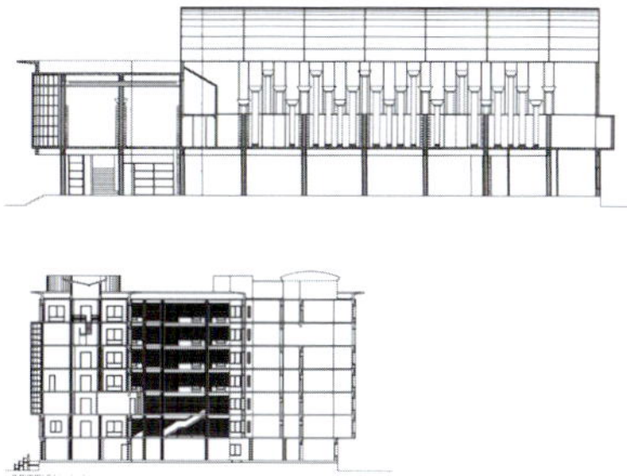

Sections

was a member of the team that won first prize in the Mujibnagar Memorial national design competition. He was also active in the now-defunct Chetana, an architectural study group that championed critical, multidisciplinary dialogues on the design culture of the country.

The building program was ambitious, requiring multiple entry points, a large number of classrooms, art and music rooms, teachers' rooms, office and administrative spaces, laboratories, a library, a cafeteria, and an indoor multipurpose hall. Most important, Ahmed wanted to incorporate an outdoor area for playing games or gathering. The main challenge for the school authority was to foster a sense of community among students, teachers, administrators, and support staff. Enabling all to congregate in *one* space was a rarity in an overpopulated and built-up city.

The goal was to develop an inspiring learning environment based on interaction, openness, sustainable climatic adaptation,

and a healthy relationship between indoor and outdoor spaces. Scholastica incorporated subject-based classrooms, which was a novel departure from the prevalent practice of local schools. This approach allowed students to move from class to class, according to the subjects in their curriculum, rather than having teachers instruct a "static" group of students, assigned to a particular classroom. The concept promoted a kinetic, interactive, and inclusive learning environment.

Architect Jalal Ahmed proposed an ingenuous solution for the constricted site: a continuous building mass of seven floors wrapped around a central courtyard, with a two-story cafeteria/multipurpose hall to the north. Scholastica recalls a host of traditional typologies, such as the vernacular Bengali courtyard house (*maidan*), or an inward-looking Mediterranean villa with a central courtyard. The open-to-the-sky hub is surrounded by an uninterrupted loop of corridors on three sides and the cafeteria on the north, ensuring a fluid congruity of indoor and outdoor spaces. Traffic-rich verandah-corridors surrounding the courtyard, as well as adjacent staircases, provide a lively social ambiance. The open-floor cafeteria on the ground level to the north extends into the courtyard, creating a fluid space, across the north-south axis.

The spatial distribution of the school carefully responds to the urban context, while the street façade evokes the impression of an educational institution. The location of the main north-south thoroughfare on the east prompted the architect to place the academic wing with the classrooms on the west, with administrative offices on the east. Not only does this arrangement significantly reduce vehicular noise in the classrooms, but it also allows the teachers to open windows for natural ventilation. There are two main public entrances on the east: One leads to the

double-height, open-floor atrium, and the other leads to the vestibule connecting the multipurpose hall on the second floor. The spacious corridor along the southern side of this hall serves as an elevated viewing gallery for the basketball court in the courtyard. In general, corridors and various staircases become social space, rather than service space.

Organizationally, Jalal Ahmed's design reflects the influence of the architects he examines: Alvar Aalto's Säynätsalo Town Hall, in Finland, and James Stirling's Staatsgalerie, in Stuttgart, Germany. As in Aalto's and Stirling's work, the courtyard at Scholastica weaves all of the spaces together, contributing to the experience of a continuous space. Although the plan follows a rectangular order, the spaces on the southern edge tilt to create interesting pockets of space that facilitate social interaction.

The street façade along the main thoroughfare articulates an organic urban image of multiplicity by its use of breaks, plastered walls, glass blocks, and reinforced concrete columns. And, the projecting roof parasol acts as a climatic device to protect the building shell from rain. One way or the other, the street façade evokes the impression of an educational institution. The overall ambiance of the school is of a continuous and delightful interplay of indoor and outdoor spaces, a quality that also nurtures open inquiries as the bedrock of meaningful education.

16. GRAMEENPHONE CORPORATE HEADQUARTERS (GP HOUSE)

LOCATION: Bashundhara, Baridhara, Dhaka 1229
ARCHITECTS: Mustapha Khalid Palash and Mohammad Foyez Ullah, of Vistaara Architects (Pvt.) Ltd.; K. M. Saiful Kader, of Icon Architects Ltd.
CONSULTANTS: Consortium of Vistaara Architects (Pvt.) Ltd. and Icon Architects Ltd.
CONSTRUCTION: 2006–2009

PRACTICAL INFORMATION:

Grameenphone corporate headquarters (GP House) is a private property and, therefore, not open to the public. Permission is required to visit the premises.

13B S. A. Residence
13C Karim Residence
16 Grameenphone Corporate Headquarters (GP House)
20 Akash Prodip Apartment Complex

According to a 2014 estimate, 75 percent of Bangladesh's 160 million people use cell phones. And, among them, more than 50 million subscribe to Grameenphone, the country's largest mobile phone service provider. Launched in 1997, it is a joint venture of Telenor (Norway's largest telecommunications company) and Grameen Telecom Corporation, a subsidiary of Grameen Bank, the renowned microfinance organization of Bangladesh. In 2005, both stakeholders acknowledged that Grameenphone's large workforce and robust footprint in the telecom market of Bangladesh warranted an accessible and efficient headquarters in Dhaka. The goal was to project a socially responsible and environmentally conscious corporate identity through the language of the architecture. Such design aspirations had earlier motivated the construction of Telenor's headquarters at Fornebu, in suburban Oslo, Norway.

Grameenphone acquired about 0.81 ha (2 acres) in Bashundhara, a planned gridiron neighborhood in northeast Dhaka, not far from the city's diplomatic zone. It is predominantly residential, with a few educational, corporate, and health care buildings. The quasi-square, trapezoidal site is flat, and its access is from the north, where the urban character is more commercial than residential. In the midst of growing urban hustle and bustle, the project's primary challenge was to balance the small-scale residential fabric with the demands of a corporate commercial center.

An international design competition was held for the future Grameenphone corporate headquarters (GP House), in 2005–2006. Three Bangladeshi and two overseas architecture firms made the short list from a pool of 501 submissions, based on their architectural design, as well as its user value and cost. The jury comprised architects from Norway, among other countries, and awarded the project to Mustapha Khalid Palash and Mohammad Foyez Ullah, of Vistaara Architects, and K. M. Saiful Kader, of Icon Architects. All three are graduates of the Bangladesh University of Engineering and Technology (BUET), in Dhaka. Considered one of the pioneers of contemporary architecture in Bangladesh, Mustapha Khalid Palash's other work includes Bashundhara City Mall; the Westin Hotel, in Dhaka; and the Radisson Blu Chittagong Bay View Hotel.

A number of considerations guided the project proposal. First, they wanted a

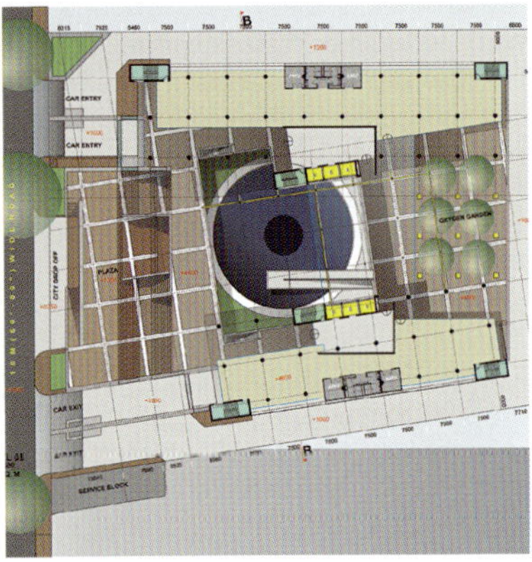

Plan: level 2

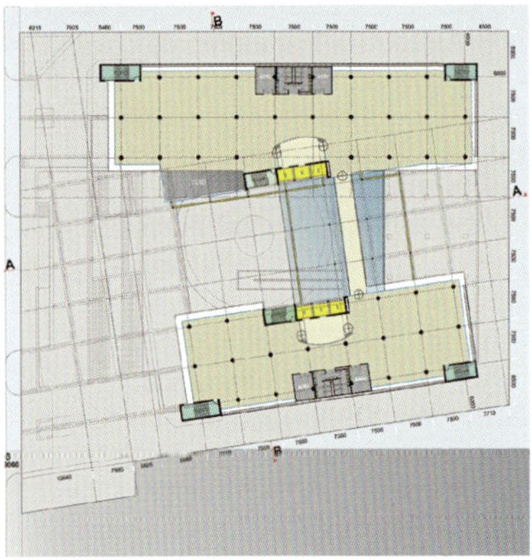

Plan: levels 4 to 6

non-hierarchical work environment, to inspire workers' creativity. Second, the work environment needed to blend with the civic realm, to create an inclusive socio-urban gesture. And, third, environmental sustainability had to be an integral part of broader corporate responsibility.

Volumetrically, the architects based the design concept on two separate asymmetric rectangular wings, connected by a spacious multilevel courtyard that acts as a public access plaza, as well as a visual connector for the entire building complex. Boldly jutting out to the northern street scene, the two wings provide open-floor workstations for approximately 2,600 Grameenphone employees. The alignment of the wings along the north-south axis allows southern light to penetrate deep into the plaza. Above the northern garden plaza, an auditorium links the two volumes, with bridges connecting every level above it. The eastern wing and bridges contain pockets of double-height, plant-filled

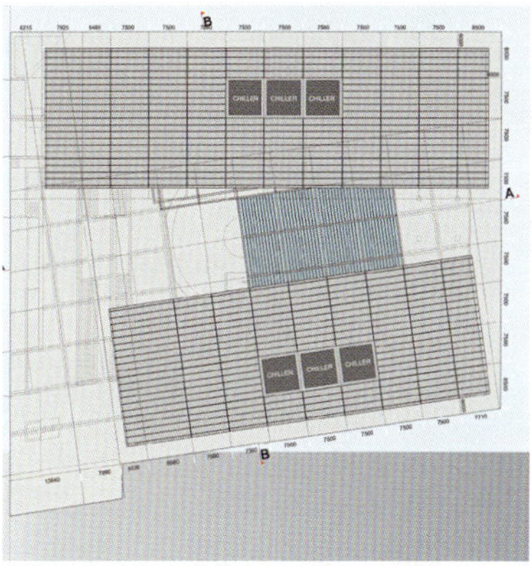

Roof plan

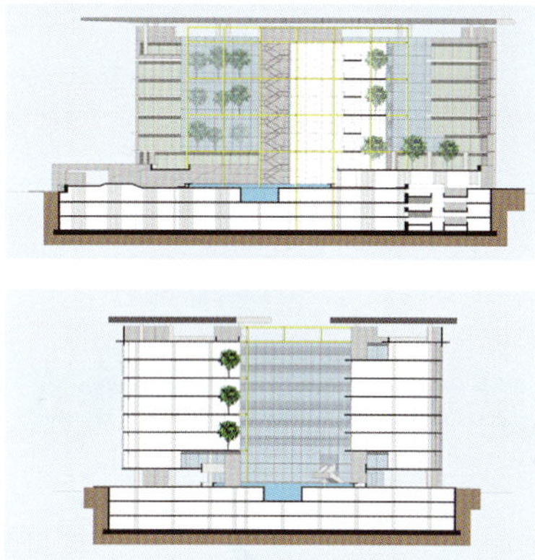

Sections

gardens on alternate floors, amplifying the relationship between indoors and outdoors. These spatial pockets also provide informal meeting areas for employees.

Access to the courtyard on the northern street side has been ingeniously split into two levels. The upper level accommodates general pedestrian access, while the lower level provides vehicular entry to the building. Three levels of underground parking address the acute traffic congestion. The total built area of GP House is 27,285 sq. m (293,693 sq. ft.). Of the allocated space (24,154.79 sq. m or 260,000 sq. ft.), it is interesting that 60 percent is for offices, while 40 percent is for parking.

The courtyard expresses two layers of symbolism. First, it suggests the vernacular organization of a courtyard house. And, second, the heart of the courtyard is a circular "pond." This is a modern articulation of a traditional Bengali topographical feature, the dugout, which provides the soil for an elevated foundation on which

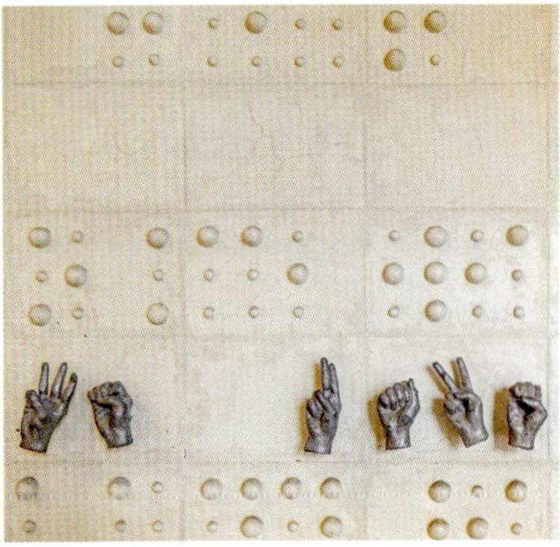

the rural hut is placed. The GP House's hydrological allegory seems to derive from the riverine geography of deltaic Bengal. However, the center of the pond does not feature a playful fountain, thrusting its water upward. Rather, it's a circular puncture that choreographs an internal cascade of water. Perhaps, the architects symbolically prioritized introspection over visual delight, as the motive for the building's overall spatial program. Furthermore, by harvesting rainwater, the aquatic courtyard combines the spiritual and aesthetic values of water with a larger mission of environmental sustainability.

The transparency and juxtaposition of the building's two wings create a simultaneously inward and outward spatial ambiance. Glazed lifts and open stairs align with the connecting bridges, further reinforcing the wings' unobstructed visual negotiation and increasing the functional flexibility in the building volumes. With a single 75 m (246 ft.) horizontal sweep,

the metal roof parasols over the two wings conjure up the image of a traditional hut and its projecting eaves. These parasols function as climatic devices, protecting the building shell from rain. The roof is split into two layers: A metal shield floats above a concrete slab, channeling a flow of cool air in between, enhancing the building's passive thermal performance.

The GP House also serves as a venue for the local art scene. Artwork and murals wrap the entire interior of the building, particularly the lobby. This corporate atrium provides exhibition space to showcase local artists' work. Dhali Al Mamoon's mural *Silent Communique* —a vast collection of hand gestures (sign language)—depicts non-verbal communication. Al Mamoon's work presents an ironic, but rich, metaphor for a company that sells a modern technology for verbal communication. Wakilur Rahman's *Shobdobhumi* (Soundscape), a steel mural comprising the names of villages in Bangladesh, has been conceived as a "linguistic geography of Bangladesh." This mural expresses a dynamic tension between the globalization of telecommunications and the phenomenology of local geography.

The overall impression of the GP House is that of a transparent collegial work environment, facilitated by abundant light, the cascading sound of water, and a non-hierarchical spatial distribution. It sets a new paradigm for corporate headquarters in Bangladesh by bringing together a sense of open access and environmental sustainability, as well as a sophisticated modernist aesthetic. Design strategies like wastewater treatment, energy-efficient artificial illumination, and passive ventilation take the building's environmental performance to a level that has rarely been achieved in the local construction industry. Whether or not "corporate responsibility" is currently in vogue, this concept attains a credible physical expression at the GP House.

17. BRAC–AARONG COMMERCIAL CENTER

LOCATION: Plot 7, Jashimuddin Avenue, Sector 3, Uttara, Dhaka 1230
ARCHITECTS: Patrick D'Rozario, Tamanna Sayeed, and Selim Altaf Biplob, of Synthesis Architects
CONSTRUCTION: 2007–2010

PRACTICAL INFORMATION:

BRAC–Aarong commercial center is open from 10 am to 8 pm every day of the week except Wednesday.

Phone: +88-02-7911652

URL: www.aarong.com

15 Scholastica School
17 BRAC–Aarong Commercial Center

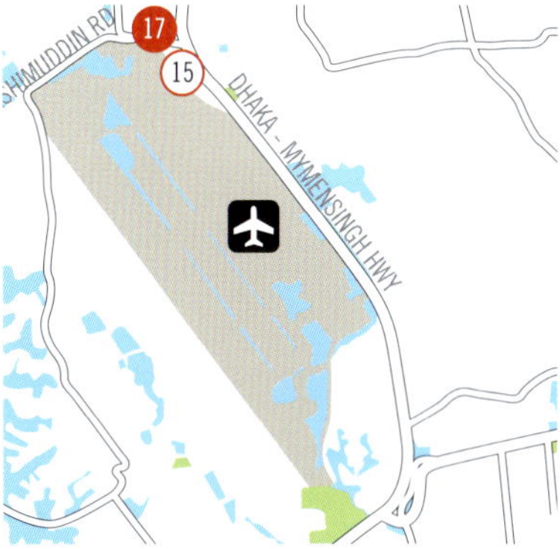

Immediately north of the Dhaka International Airport is the nine-story BRAC–Aarong Commercial Center, one of a handful of contemporary modernist buildings that symbolize the architectural vibrancy of the sprawling neighborhood of Uttara. Aarong is the flagship, socially responsive enterprise of Bangladesh Rehabilitation Assistance Committee (BRAC; formerly known as the Bangladesh Rural Advancement Committee). Established in 1978, the retail chain Aarong stimulated the local economy through bottom-up enterprises, by revitalizing the handicraft industry, encouraging self-help entrepreneurship, and providing employment opportunities, particularly in rural areas. Today, in popular reckoning, Aarong is synonymous with a stylish urban shopping mall that had significant economic trickle-down effects on rural artisans and suppliers.

Founded by Sir Fazle Hasan Abed, BRAC is generally considered the world's largest non-governmental organization (NGO), based on the number of employees and people it serves. In 1972, after the liberation war of Bangladesh, BRAC started out as a relief operation, when refugees began returning to the newly independent country. Soon, its scope of work broadened to serve people suffering from illness, poverty, illiteracy, and lack of social justice. Focusing on such vital social sectors as microfinance, education, health care, legal services, community empowerment, and social enterprises, BRAC advanced a crucial development agenda in Bangladesh and many other countries around the world.

As one of BRAC's social initiatives, Aarong's purpose was to bolster the local economy, while generating urban consumers' interest in high-quality handicrafts and traditional artifacts reimagined with a modern twist. Aarong now has branches across the country, including all major cities in Bangladesh. And, it is contributing to the revival of the handicraft industry, which, in recent times, had been threatened by cheap factory-made products. Over the years, there are indications that Aarong has helped to create job opportunities among disenfranchised rural women in Bangladesh. Furthermore, Aarong is a pioneer in making traditional products hip and cosmopolitan, including fabric, embroidery, dresses, jewelry, wall mats, pottery, toys, metalwork, leather goods, candles, handmade paper, shoes, quilts, and furniture. Today, Aarong is viewed as an indispensable destination for those seeking artistic products and souvenirs.

Patrick D'Rozario, Tamanna Sayeed, and Selim Altaf Biplob, of Synthesis Architects, a Dhaka-based architectural firm, designed Aarong's Uttara branch. The Bengali word *aarong* means a "village fair" or "market." In the pastoral setting of rural Bangladesh, a village fair typically takes place on the riverbank, in an area marked by one or two large trees. And, the site is generally accessible by both land and water. The spatial organization of the village fair—in which people move along an informal corridor, from stall to stall, or from product to product—inspired the architects. The Aarong building reimagines this corridor as a grand flight of steps connecting all of the floors. Called a Celebration Stair, these broad steps evoke the experience of a public gathering at village fair.

The site is narrow, measuring only 16.76 m (55 ft.) wide. However, the building's strategic location at the turn of the road affords it a bold presence on Uttara's skyline. The building is divided vertically into two parts.

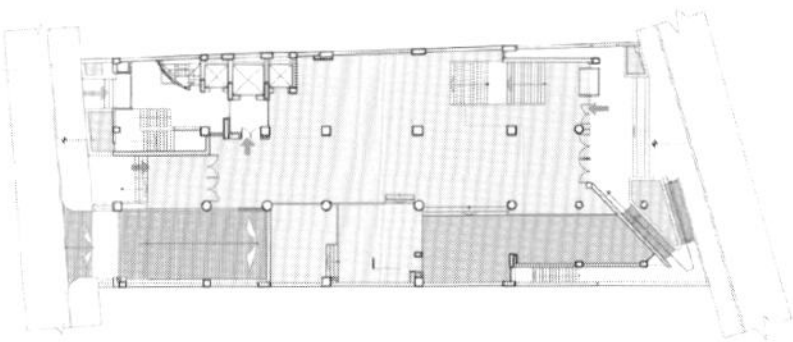

Ground floor plan

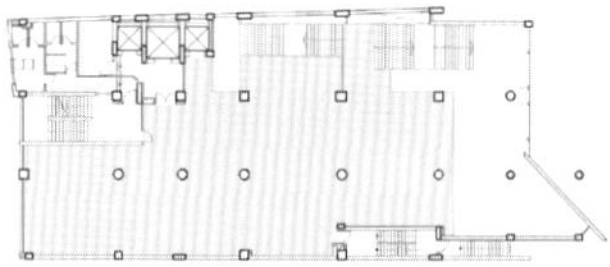

1st floor plan

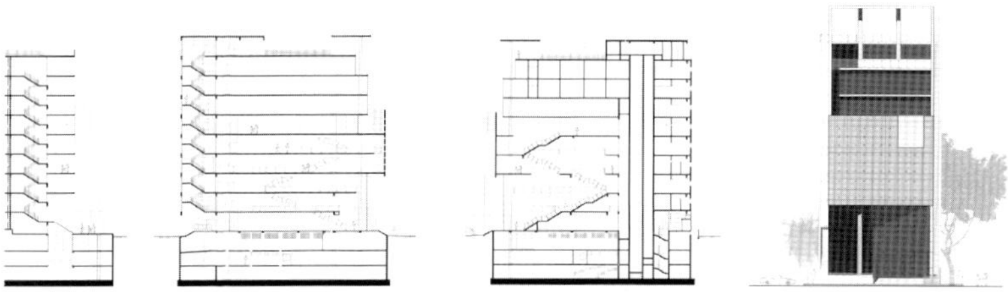

Sections and front elevation

The first six floors provide continuously interlinked retail spaces. The remaining three floors serve as a hotel, which BRAC owns and operates. (The architects had originally earmarked these three levels for office space). On the sixth floor, a restaurant called Shororeetu serves both hotel guests and outside patrons. The roof is designed as an outdoor theater, where traditional cultural festivities could take place. Additionally, there are three levels below grade that accommodate parking and building services.

The front façade of BRAC-Aarong Commercial Center comprises two elements. One is a mid-level projecting plane, marked by a grid of perforations and the Aarong sign, which is parallel to Airport Road, the city's primary north-south thoroughfare. The façade's base plane features a lofty canopy roof that is divided into three bays, by two circular columns, and aligns with the north-south axis. The two intersecting planes create a recessed and inviting entrance consisting of a triple-height glass

façade and an wall. Two ramps along that wall provide access.

Once inside, the visitor faces an open ground floor, showcasing merchandise and the broad stairway leading to the floors above, each devoted to similar product types. A vast wall mural connects the vertical shaft of the staircase. As the building section illustrates, the staircase introduces a kinetic personality to the interior. This is an atrium with movement. Natural light is highly controlled in the interior to protect the often colorful artifacts and fabrics. The architects have incorporated solar panels that support 8 percent to 10 percent of the building's total electrical requirements.

As if to replicate the quality of handicraft detail, the building's construction and interior present a tactile sensibility by means of concrete joints, glass details, and intricate woodwork. From the street, Aarong Uttara resembles a magnified handicraft, rendered with an aesthetic of minimalist modernism and cautiously dramatized by an interplay of shifting façades and a perforated plane. This interplay of planes also provides ample shade and protection from driving rain, while significantly reducing the building's maintenance cost.

The retail chain has acquired the cultural gravitas of a tastemaker. Many who step into an Aarong branch consider it an experience of both culture and heritage. Prior to any national or religious festival, Aarong is filled with swarms of shoppers. At Aarong Uttara, an aura of cultural pride and nationalistic consumerism pervades the architecture, as well. It has garnered awards from the Institute of Architects Bangladesh, Berger, and J. K. Cement Ltd. (India).

18. MUSEUM OF INDEPENDENCE AND INDEPENDENCE MONUMENT

LOCATION: Suhrawardi Udyan Road,
Kazi Nazrul Islam Avenue, Dhaka 1000
ARCHITECTS: Marina Tabassum and Kashef Mahboob Chowdhury
CONSTRUCTION: 1999–2015

PRACTICAL INFORMATION:

Visitors may tour the Museum of Independence and Independence Monument. There is an entry fee. See "Information for the Visitor," p. 159, for details.

4 Curzon Hall
5 Faculty of Fine Arts
6 Teacher–Student Center (TSC)
9 Department of Architecture Building
18 Museum of Independence and Independence Monument

NEARBY ATTRACTION:

A Ramna Park

The complex comprising the Museum of Independence and Independence Monument sits on a historic site in Dhaka, central to Bangladesh's national consciousness. It is located inside Suhrawardi Udyan, formerly a colonial-era racecourse and now one of Dhaka's few remaining urban parks. The museum and the monument recall not only the traumatic history of the country's independence war, but also two pivotal events that spanned the duration of the hostilities between the two wings of Pakistan.

Here, Bangladesh's nationalist leader Sheikh Mujibur Rahman, popularly known as Bangabandhu, delivered his historic speech on March 7, 1971, triggering East Pakistan's struggle for emancipation. His 11-minute oration, enshrined as Bangladesh's own Gettysburg Address—"The struggle this time is for emancipation! The struggle this time is for independence"—mobilized a nation in its determined pursuit of self-rule. This is also the historic location where the Pakistani army officially surrendered to the combined forces of Bangladesh and India in December 1971, ending a genocidal campaign unleashed on the people of East Pakistan. The new nation of Bangladesh emerged thereafter.

From the beginning, the museum and the monument had to shoulder a collective burden of capturing an architectural language that would simultaneously mourn, reminisce, introspect, and look forward and upward. And, in 1997, a national architectural competition solicited designs for these commemorative edifices. The jury included a group of prominent Bangladeshi architects, engineers, academics, and an artist. Among them were Muzharul Islam, Shamsul Wares, Rabiul Hussain, Meer Mobashsher Ali, Jamilur Reza Choudhury, Muntasir Mamun, and Hashem Khan. The architects of the winning entry were Marina Tabassum, Kashef Mahboob Chowdhury, and A. K. M. Sirajuddin (who later left the team under unclear circumstances). All three graduated from the Department of Architecture, at at the Bangladesh University of Engineering and Technology (BUET), during the mid-1990s.

Presenting their project less as a building and more as an urban landscape, the architects embraced a monastically austere design attitude to articulate the momentous significance of Bangladesh's liberation war, as well as the challenges of Dhaka as a very congested place with an

Basement level

Site plan

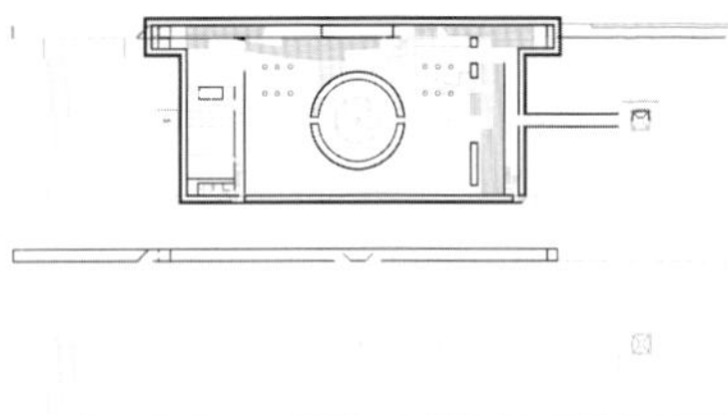

Plans: plaza and museum

acute shortage of green spaces. The dual commitments led them to conceive a museum and monument complex, comprising 27.11 ha (67 acres), that had very little building activity above ground, to minimize any ecological disruption of Suhrawardi Udyan. Taking their architecture below ground, the architects proposed a lyrical narrative of descent into the earth's womb, a return to the primordial cave, choreographing a spatial story that inspires more introspection and less patriotism.

A groundbreaking example, the project proposed the country's first subterranean museum, a bold undertaking in a deltaic, tropical country with considerable annual rainfall. Above ground, there is only a linear public plaza (a concrete slab, 45.72 cm or 18 in. thick) that acts as the roof of the underground museum, accessible from a circular plaza in Suhrawardi Udyan's western periphery. The plaza itself is set within a rectangular body of water and, eventually, within an elliptical landscape.

Museum gallery

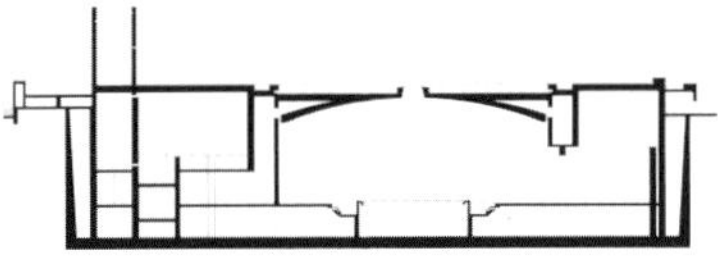

Section

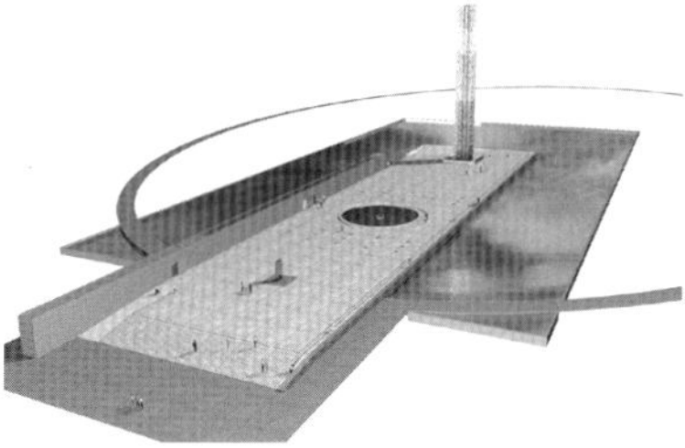

Aerial render

The horizontal sweep of the entire ensemble is broken only twice: first, by the long freestanding wall along the northern edge of the plaza and, second, by the 45.72 m (150 ft.) high Independence Monument (Swadhinata Stambha), to which the whole complex gravitates. The tower's symbolism is unmistakable: It is a beacon of light to enlighten the nation. A mediated dualism of light (the tower) and darkness (the museum cave), all set in an urban meadow, provides an architectural foil for contemplating the meaning of independence. By proposing little building activity on the ground, the museum offers the nation a pilgrimage site without a shrine. British architect David Adjaye calls the project an "anti-icon," a sort of non-building that composes invisibility as a meditative building program.

The construction of the US$25 million project began in 1999 and was eventually completed in 2015, enduring both periodic delays and financial hiatus,

Rotunda and water column

perpetuated by the change of government and bureaucratic entanglements. Yet, upon completion, the museum and monument created a novel architectural tapestry, weaving together above and below, interior and exterior, light and darkness, land and water—all part of a poignant national story told in an atmosphere of quiet, serene grandeur.

The visitor enters the underground museum through a door located at the middle of the long wall. A ramp descends into the museum proper. At the center, there is a rotunda, the architectural protagonist in a chiaroscuro theater of sequential spaces. While some spaces are consciously empty, others display images of genocide, torture, and other war sagas. A grid of skylights pierces the concrete ceiling over the double-height gallery. The influence of Louis Kahn is palpable, while the likes of Peter Zumthor and Alvaro Siza whisper their minimalist stories.

The central rotunda appears to be a spartan temple of light and shade, an ancient naos or a *garbh griha*, culminating in a

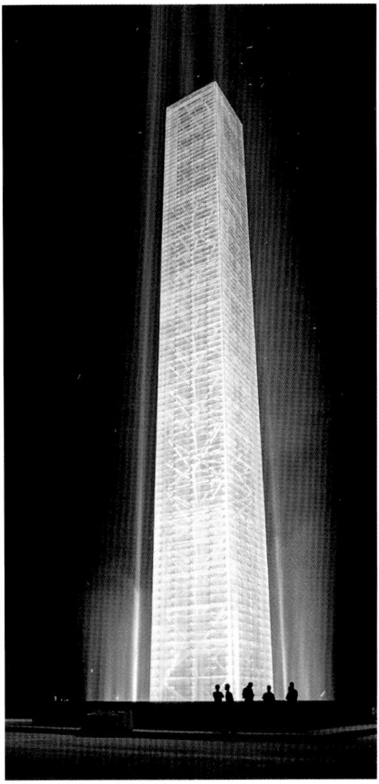

Independence Monument

luminous water column streaming down from the circular pool that sits axially at the plaza level. Visitors are expected to circumambulate the underground pool, recalling the experience of going around the Maha Stupa of Sanchi, the Buddhist monastery in India's Madhya Pradesh, except that here, a translucent liquid *stambha* (column) replaces the sacred hemispherical mound. As if tears from the Pantheon's oculus, this water column flows into the rotunda's pool, cut concentrically within a three-tiered recess. Alluding to the hydro-ecological character of the Bengal delta, water at the symbolic center of the rotunda seems to inspire spiritual reckoning, cleansing, and soul-searching.

The subterranean museum includes a 155-seat auditorium. The entry to and exit from the museum form a circular journey, starting from and ending at the plaza. All the while, the Independence Monument directs, orients, and lifts. Originally intended as a tower of stacked glass panels, able to refract light, the monument was eventually built as a space frame, sheathed in glass panels, requiring illumination at night.

Approaching the monument from the west, the visitor experiences a visual story of the liberation war, narrated by a terracotta mural that almost spans the entire length of the plaza's northern wall. The mural also includes quotes from various Bengali poets.

Together, the Museum of Independence and Independence Monument seem to capture the land-water mysticism of deltaic Bengal. Yet, a visitor can also experience the evocative expansiveness of a Roman forum or the geological assemblage of an Egyptian mastaba sanctuary. A range of experiential possibilities allow the museum and the monument complex to transcend the weight of seeking nativist identities. As people from all walks of life congregate here to spend a pleasant time, the glass obelisk signals the advent of a new type of urban culture in which patriotism, nationalism, and cosmopolitanism coalesce.

19. KRISHIBID INSTITUTION OF BANGLADESH (KIB)

LOCATION: Krishi Khamar Sarak, Farmgate, Dhaka 1215
ARCHITECTS: Iqbal Habib, Ishtiaque Zahir Titas, and Nayara Nuary Islam, of Vitti Sthapati Brindo Ltd.
CONSTRUCTION: 2011–2014

PRACTICAL INFORMATION:

Visitors can make arrangements to tour the Krishibid Institution of Bangladesh (KIB), which is open from 9 am to 5 pm, Sunday to Thursday.

Contact:
Vitti Sthapati Brindo Ltd.
27/A Shangshad Avenue, Dhaka 1215

Phone: +88-02-8143471
or +88-01-912888001
E-Mail: vittibd@gmail.com

8 National Assembly Building (Jatiyo Shangshad Bhaban)
10 Bangladesh Agricultural Research Council (BARC) Headquarters
19 Krishibid Institution of Bangladesh (KIB)

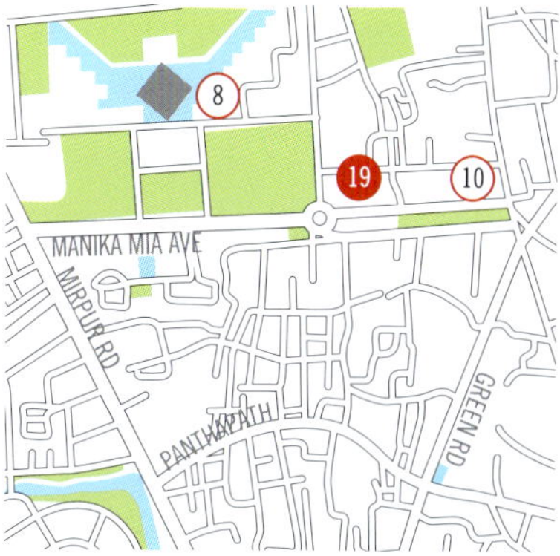

The Krishibid Institution of Bangladesh (KIB) near Farmgate, one of Dhaka's busiest urban nodes, offers a useful insight into the challenges and emerging aspirations of designing public-sector buildings in Bangladesh. On the one hand, there is a bureaucratic government organization with enthusiastic but archaic design expectations of what an institutional building should look like and how to build it. On the other hand, there are architects who would be willing to negotiate the bureaucratic maze to produce a public-oriented aspirational building. In the end, it is mostly a collaborative work.

The sponsor of KIB is the government's Department of Agricultural Extension, an organization that originated during the British colonial times. In the wake of the great famine of 1862–1865, the Famine Commission first recommended the creation of a Department of Agriculture, to provide administrative oversight to this sector. And, in 1870, the Department of Agriculture was formed within the purview of the Revenue Department. More than 30 years later, in 1906, an independent Department of Agriculture was established. At the same time, 404.69 ha (1,000 acres) of land on the northern edge of the city—including the present-day Farmgate and the Parliament area—were allocated to develop an agricultural farm and laboratory, along with areas for experimental agriculture. Since then, the organization underwent many changes and expansions throughout the 20th century.

However, after Bangladesh emerged as a new nation, too many uncoordinated programs and different government messages related to agricultural extension adversely affected the lives of peasants in the field. As a result, in 1982, the Government of Bangladesh created a comprehensive organization called Krishi Shomprosharon Odhidoptor (Department of Agricultural Extension), to provide effective needs-based services to peasants of all strata. The key objective is to ensure a streamlined administrative and knowledge-based environment in which peasants can best harness their lands, contributing not only to the agricultural sector, but also to the socioeconomic development of the country. Having received government funds to create an administrative facility, the Department of Agricultural Extension commissioned the design of KIB.

Iqbal Habib, Ishtiaque Zahir Titas, and Nayara Nuary Islam, of the Dhaka-based

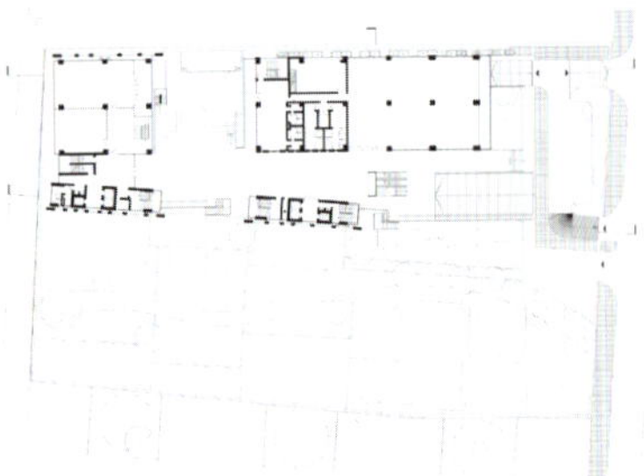

Ground floor plan

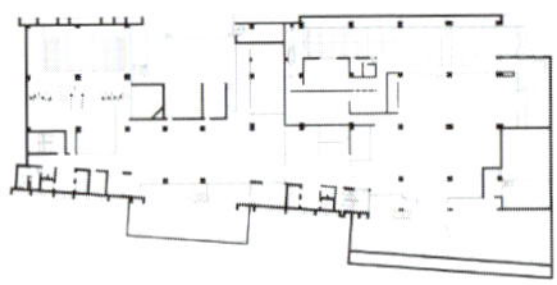

Basement plan

firm Vitti Sthapati Brindo Ltd., envisioned a public-oriented building based on an "open society" ethos, sustainability, and, most of all, cultural idioms. Unlike conventional government buildings with a highly controlled single entry, KIB opens its arms to the public with an architectural gesture of welcome, amply demonstrated by the quality of public accessibility and the kinds of spaces at the ground level.

The linear site along the north-south axis opens to a busy one-way street from the south. Once inside, a spacious pedestrian ramp leads to a public plaza, connected to a 500-person multipurpose community center, tucked under the boldly projecting auditorium. As the hub of community gathering at KIB, the auditorium is the most prominent form visible from the street and establishes the civic identity of the entire complex. The 1,000-seat auditorium is directly accessible from the public plaza through a compact vestibule, which is also the beginning of a

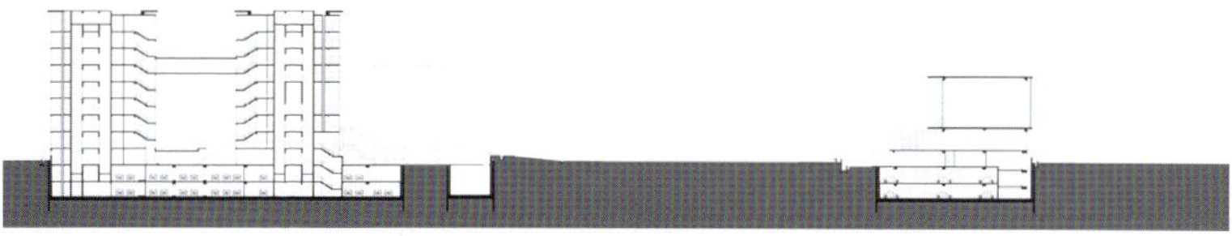

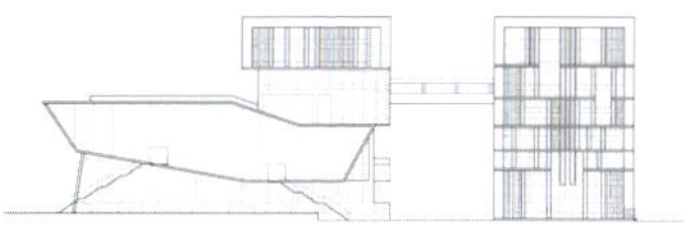

Elevation

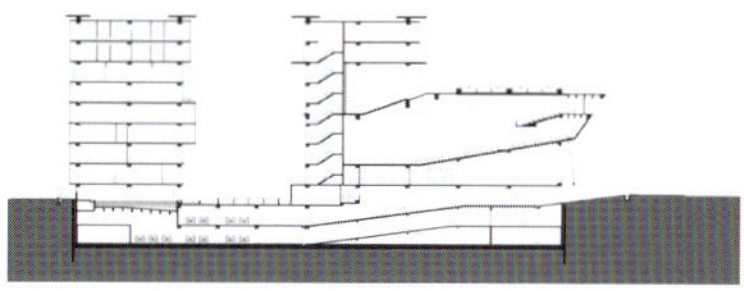

Sections

linear spine of steps parallel to this venue, providing access to its different levels of seating.

The Department of Agricultural Extension wanted the architects of KIB to celebrate three basic elements in their design: *krishok* (peasant), *krishibid* (agriculturalist), and the architectural tradition of Bangladesh. The architects, in turn, sought to incorporate these components by abstracting them through a modernist language of architecture. They resisted the lure of viewing the figure of the peasant and a pastoral world as readily available visual symbols. Rather, the architects demonstrated a sensible restraint by seeking to understand the horizontal sweep of deltaic Bengal and how it could become an architectural program in a tight urban setting.

A choreographed movement from the public to private zones, interspersed with "breathing spaces" (*uthan*), recalls the spatial progression in traditional mosque

or temple architecture. Considering the urban challenges of the site—particularly how to approach a linear plot from a major thoroughfare—the architects prioritized a liberal provision of unobstructed pedestrian access to the complex as KIB's symbolic frame.

Morphologically, three basic forms populate 42 percent of the linear site along the north-south axis: the auditorium, plus the southern and the northern building blocks. The southern block is public domain, with the auditorium jutting out from it obliquely, like a wedge-shaped canopy. The northern block houses institutional activities, including a library, research facilities, classrooms, seminar rooms, a training center, and a dormitory. There is also an independent recreational club, along with a sizable swimming pool at the grade level. The complex has two levels of underground parking.

A stepped courtyard and skywalk connect the pair of eight-story building blocks, while a continuous public promenade at the plaza level extends all the way to the north. The open-to-the-sky courtyard in the canyon between the building blocks brings the public into the heart of the site. Evoking the spatial experience of a riverside market in rural Bengal, the courtyard punctuates the building masses with a patch of green and the sky above it. The western half of the linear site is a tapestry of urban gardens.

The rectilinear site gains much heat from the scorching afternoon sun. On the western façades, the architects mitigated this typical problem by creating deep recesses filled with vertical louvers temper the fierce tropical sun. A screen comprising tall wooden louvers protects the auditorium proper from direct heat gain, an emblematic architectural device that the Mughals employed to shade their pavilions. Additional inspiration for this type of layered space comes from Louis Kahn's National Assembly (Parliament) building, within walking distance of KIB.

More broadly, the architecture of KIB continues a historic typology of institutional complexes, best exemplified by Le Corbusier's unbuilt project for the U.S.S.R.'s Palace of the Soviets (1928–1931) and by Lucio Costa and Oscar Niemeyer's Ministry of Education and Health (1937–1943), in Rio de Janeiro. These buildings formally differentiate the

public congregation area, such as the auditorium, as a way of creating both spatial volumes and the architectural personality of the building complex. Bangladeshi architect Bashirul Haq reimagined this typology in his Bangladesh Chemical Industries Corporation (BCIC) headquarters, in downtown Dhaka.

Despite some awkward details—perhaps the result of its ultra-speedy construction time—the US$15 million KIB is a bold step forward in the annals of the country's institutional buildings. A visitor to KIB is reminded that maintenance is an essential, yet overlooked, component. The institution's ill maintenance is not a fault of the architects, but rather evidence of a misguided bureaucratic culture that does not accommodate a building's graceful aging as part of its budget. In the end, however, the architectural experience of KIB is uplifting.

20. AKASH PRODIP APARTMENT BUILDING

LOCATION: Plot 46, Road 25, Block A, Banani Residential Area, Dhaka 1213
ARCHITECTS: Nahas Ahmed Khalil and Mahbub Hossain
LANDSCAPE ARCHITECT: Jubair Hasan
CONSTRUCTION: 2010–2015

PRACTICAL INFORMATION:

The Akash Prodip apartment building is a private property and, therefore, not open to the public. Visitors might receive special permission to tour the premises by contacting the project architects.

13B S. A. Residence
13C Karim Residence
16 Grameenphone Corporate Headquarters (GP House)
20 Akash Prodip Apartment Building

NEARBY ATTRACTION:

A Gulshan Society Mosque
(Architect: Kashef Mahboob Chowdhury)

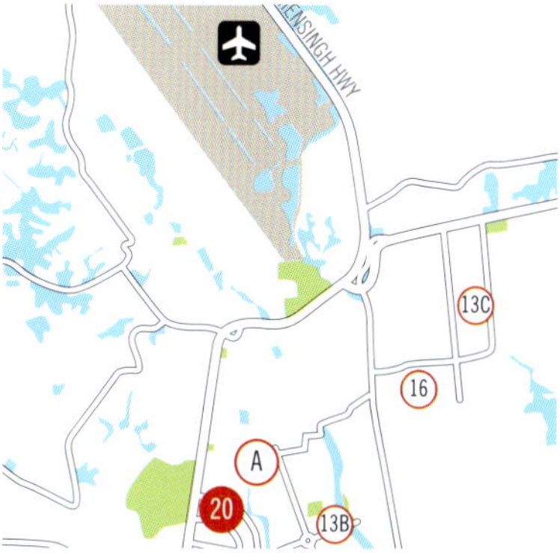

Located in Banani, one of Dhaka's upscale planned residential areas, Akash Prodip is a multifamily apartment building designed by architects Nahas Ahmed Khalil and Mahbub Hossain. Even though it represents a residential typology common since the early 1990s, Akash Prodip also signals the emergence of the next generation of apartment buildings in the capital city's private-sector real estate development.

In 2006, the introduction of the Floor Area Ratio building code reduced a building's footprint within a plot, thereby increasing the city's aggregate open spaces. Akash Prodip incorporates this code's restrictions. With only 54.75 percent ground coverage and a garden-like open ground floor plan, this apartment building encapsulates many of the emerging trends in green design. The architects and the real estate company that commissioned them seem to have found common ground where sustainable design and profit inform each other.

This was not the case a decade or so ago. Since the 1970s, Dhaka's rapidly burgeoning urban population led to a subsequent increase in demand for housing. And, private real estate companies became major urban actors with significant political clout and economic muscle. Architects typically did not have much control over the design of their commissioned housing projects. They were expected to utilize all available space, to maximize the company's profit.

Thanks to Khalil's stature as an architect, Akash Prodip heralds a new type of client-architect synergy, in which the client understands the social and monetary value of environmentally friendly design, while the architect is mindful of the client's challenges and aspirations. Thus, this apartment complex is a departure from the typical profit-motivated housing projects that had been the standard until recently. With its community-oriented common spaces, particularly at the ground level, Akash Prodip presents a user-friendly building, mediating between capital and design with welcoming results.

Residential buildings surround Akash Prodip on three sides, and it is accessible from the south. The southern façade of the building—characterized by a variegated mix of projecting terraces, fenestration variations, and handmade terra-cotta details—establishes a lively "dialogue" with the streetscape. The building accommodates 17 apartments

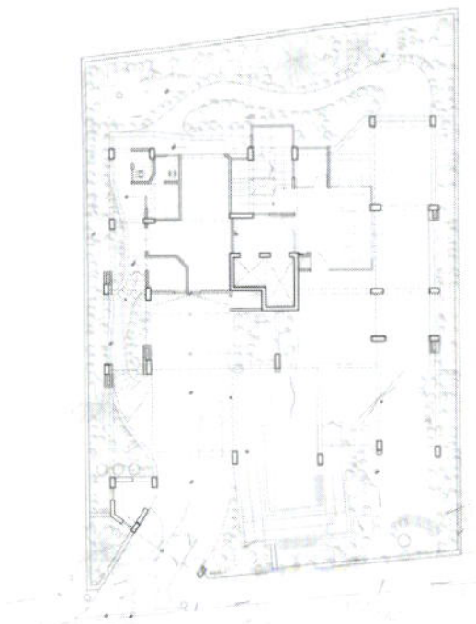

Ground floor plan

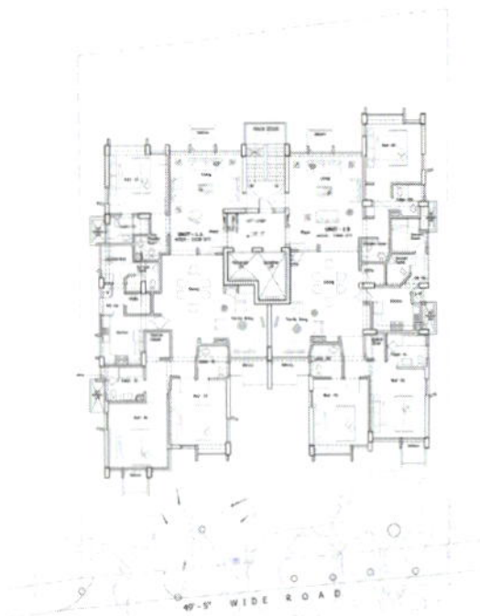

1st floor plan

within a total built area of 5,760 sq. m (62,000 sq. ft.). The typical unit size is 204.39 sq. m (2,200 sq. ft.). A gentle interplay of brick and concrete walls make the 11-story building stand out from its neighborhood.

Typical units have an entry foyer, living room, dining room, family space, kitchen with an adjacent servant area, and three bedrooms with attached bathrooms. The units attain variety by single- and double-height terraces and façade modulation with different types of shading devices. Main bedrooms are located in the south, to maximize their exposure to the southern breeze.

The entire ground floor has the feel of an urban garden as the building is lifted off the ground on columns. It is a "public square" for families and a play area for kids, a small but significant respite from the grinding daily life of the city, where public open spaces are fast disappearing. A winding walkway wraps

Elevation

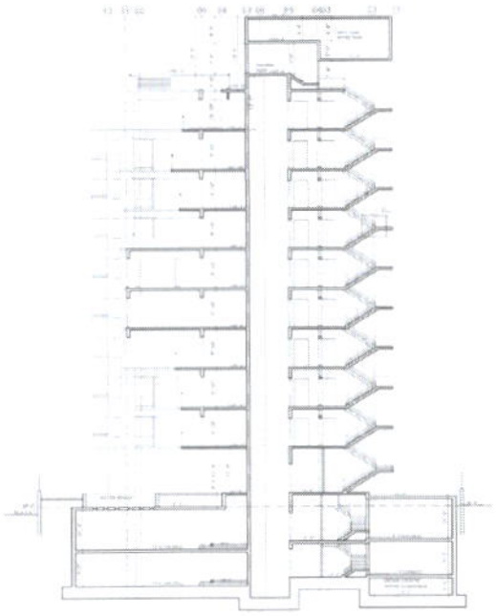

Section

the perimeter of the building, weaving through a constructed "wilderness." This walking trail can also function as a kids' biking path.

The experience of openness on the ground floor is further heightened by a garden of trees, grass, textured pavement, and water. Architect Jubair Hasan's landscape design creates a vibrant green base from which the building rises. A small pond near the main entrance serves as a symbolic marker for the country's deltaic landscape and the significance of water in it. Unlike typical apartment buildings that dominate the cityscape, there is no parking on the ground level, thus freeing up the ground floor for community usage. Parking is provided on two underground levels, despite the increase in construction cost.

Akash Prodip reflects architect Nahas Khalil's design experiments since his early career and commitment to finding an "organic identity" for architecture in

Bangladesh. He received his Bachelor of Architecture degree from the Bangladesh University of Engineering and Technology (BUET), in 1982, an era when the discourse of "critical regionalism"—as variously theorized by Kenneth Frampton, Alexander Tzonis and Liane Lefaivre, William Curtis, and Suha Ozkan—dominated architectural thinking around the world. Muzharul Islam, the patriarch of Bangladeshi architecture, also inspired many young architects to look for spatial organizations, indigenous building materials, and aesthetic qualities that would capture the spirit of a modern Bengali spatial character.

The influence of such international organizations as the Aga Khan Trust for Culture, founded in 1988, promoted regionalist architecture in Muslim-majority countries, including Bangladesh. These efforts further bolstered the discussions of architecture in the developing world published in *Mimar: Architecture in Development*, which first appeared in 1981. The generation of Nahas Khalil had found their cause. Khalil's projects—Aziz Khan Residence, Matir Bari, United International University (2003), and Chandralok (2010)—emblematized a personal search for visual and spatial expressions appropriate for the country. Akash Prodip is no exception. Carrying on that commitment, the apartment building offers a tactile, regionalist ambiance: universally modern, yet conditioned by a sophisticated local flavor.

21. BAIT UR ROUF MOSQUE

LOCATION: Faidabad (Transmitter More), Uttara, Dhaka 1230
ARCHITECT: Marina Tabassum
CONSTRUCTION: 2007–2012
AWARD: Aga Khan Award for Architecture, 2016

PRACTICAL INFORMATION:

Bait Ur Rouf mosque is open to all visitors.

21 Bait Ur Rouf Mosque

NEARBY ATTRACTION:

A Turag River

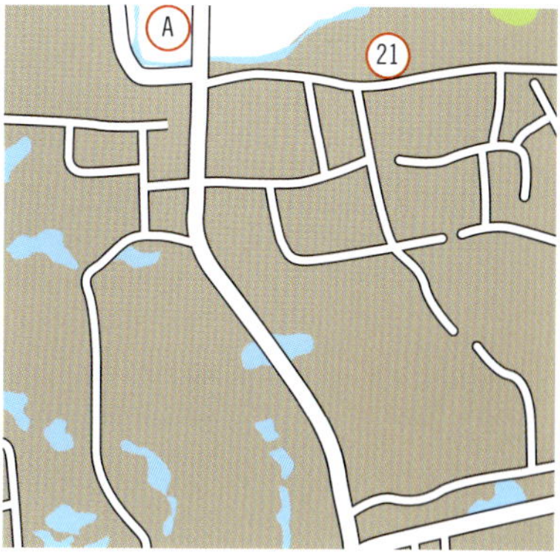

Mosques have been a dominant building typology in Bengal since the advent of Muslim rule in the region in the early 13th century. To understand architectural evolution, innovation, and adaptation in Bengal since then, one can profitably look at Bengal's mosques, dotting the entire delta. They are characterized by ambitious planning, material manifestation, and distinctive architectural features. From Ghorar mosque (15th century) at Barobazar, Jhenidah, and Shait Gambuj mosque (15th century) at Bagerhat (near Khulna) to Sat Gambuj mosque (17th century) in Dhaka, Bengal offers a fertile field of religious architecture.

It is not surprising, then, that contemporary architects in Bangladesh would continue to view mosque architecture as a prime medium for aesthetic experimentation and the search for deeper cultural meanings. Marina Tabassum is one of them. She designed Bait Ur Rouf mosque in Faidabad, Uttara, on the northern fringe of Dhaka, adjacent to the Turag River.

The monastic geometry of the mosque, its brick choreography and chiaroscuro play of interior light, and its siting in the midst of frenzied urban growth—all suggest how the architect negotiated both the region's rich legacy of mosque architecture and the poetics of minimalist modernism. Bait Ur Rouf mosque echoes the simplicity of Sultanate-era mosques, while remaining staunchly committed to an archetypal aesthetic modernity.

Bait Ur Rouf mosque is the result of community resilience. It was built with the resources mobilized by the local community that congregates here for daily and Friday prayers. The mosque's modest budget (US$150,000) dictated the selection of low-cost materials and a simplified construction technology. The architect chose brick to reduce the building's maintenance costs, which are minimal.

The original client was Sufia Khatun, who migrated with her family to East Pakistan after the Indian Partition (1947). Widowed at the age of 46, after losing her husband during the 1971 liberation war, she found herself in a precarious financial position. To provide for her family, she depended on the limited means that the family property yielded. Khatun owned 8.1 ha (20 acres) of agrarian land in the Faidabad area, which she leased to local farmers from the surrounding villages. In 2005, Khatun decided to donate part of her land to build a mosque, where the community

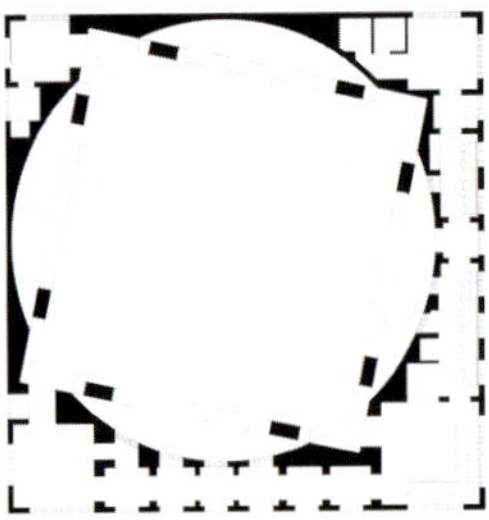

Ground floor plan

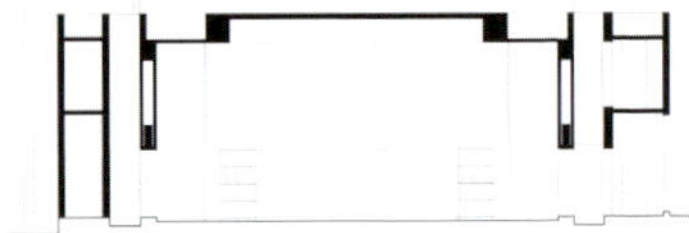

Section

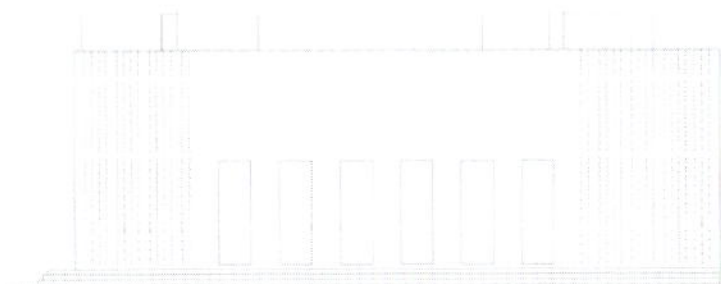

Elevation

could gather for prayer. Unfortunately, she passed away in 2006, leaving the architect (her grandchild) with the responsibility of following through on the project. Six years later, Tabassum achieved that goal.

The site is flanked by a 4.57 m (15 ft.) wide road to the west and a 2.4 m (8 ft.) wide road to the south. In many ways, the mosque is a testament to the optimism that uplifting architecture can still flourish in areas where indiscriminate, unplanned urbanization is the norm. The Faidabad area is not under the jurisdiction of the Dhaka building bylaws or the approval authority (RAJUK). Thus, the urban context of the mosque is highly dense and chaotic. The lack of land regulation and increasing demand for lower- and middle-income housing led to an urban condition characterized by congested neighborhoods with narrow alleys and inadequate community facilities. Bait Ur Rouf mosque provides a welcome respite from the banality of uncontrolled urban growth.

Because the site's axis creates a 13 degree angle with Mecca, this deviation called for an innovative layout. Three volumes are introduced, one inserted into the other, to create a sequence of spaces. The outermost volume is a square (22.9 m x 22.9 m or 75 ft. x 75 ft.), with 7.6 m (25 ft.) high walls, that parallels the road and creates the main façade of the mosque. Total combined floor area is 780 sq. m (8,396 sq. ft.). A cylindrical volume is inserted into it, allowing the rotation of the prayer hall toward Mecca and creating light courts on all four sides.

All ancillary functions, such as the entrance courts, ablution, toilet facilities, Imam's office, stairs, and a small library, are located within the space created by the outer square and inner cylindrical volume. The outer part is supported by loadbearing brick walls, while the main prayer hall, 15.24 m (50 ft.) square in plan and 10.7 m (35 ft.) in height, is a column-free space, raised on eight peripheral columns. The prayer hall can accommodate approximately 500 people, and the mosque's porous brick walls provide natural ventilation.

Bait Ur Rouf mosque is worth a visit not only for its design excellence, informed by a careful reading of history, but also for a moving experience of how architecture can galvanize a community for the greater social good. Its architecture helps elevate the daily rituals of prayer to a transcendental realm of spirituality. Described as "a refuge for spirituality in urban Dhaka," Bait Ur Rouf mosque received the prestigious Aga Khan Award for Architecture in 2016.

22. ARCHITECTURE OF SOCIAL EMPOWERMENT

22A
JAAGO FOUNDATION SCHOOL
LOCATION: 1/1 Graveyard Road, Jamaibazaar Karail, Banani, Dhaka 1213
ARCHITECT: Architecture for Humanity–Dhaka, Bangladesh (AFH–Dhaka)
DESIGN TEAM: Imrul Kayes and Rabeya Rahman, of AFH–Dhaka; Zihad Zaman, of JAAGO Foundation School
CONSTRUCTION: 2011

Visitors to JAAGO Foundation School must make prior arrangements.

Contact:
Salim Murshed, Project Officer
JAAGO Foundation School, Banani Branch

Phone: +88-01-777742814
E-Mail: salim.murshed@jaago.com.bd

22B
ARCADIA EDUCATION AND VOCATIONAL TRAINING PROJECT
LOCATION: Char Algi, Alipur, Keraniganj, Dhaka 1313
ARCHITECT: Saif Ul Haque
CONSTRUCTION: 2015

Non-governmental organizations (NGOs) are crucial actors in Bangladesh's development sector. During the past two decades or so, the country has made remarkable strides in a range of social indicators, in particular, poverty alleviation, rural development, non-formal grassroots education, village-based community health, and women's empowerment. Many observers attribute this achievement to various development initiatives by NGOs, and it is estimated that there are about 2,000 operating in Bangladesh. In addition to fostering nationwide programs, BRAC, ASA, and Proshika are among the large NGOs that are also known around the world for their bottom-up, community-driven development work.

It is not surprising that many NGOs would embrace the language of architecture as part of their development mission and a source of human-capacity building. This section discusses the architectural patronage of two NGOs—JAAGO Foundation, and Maleka Welfare Trust—and how they champion spatial innovation as one of the key catalysts of social advancement.

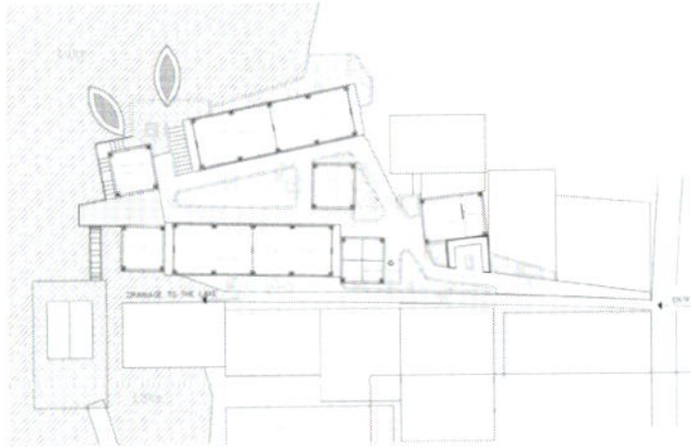

Ground floor plan

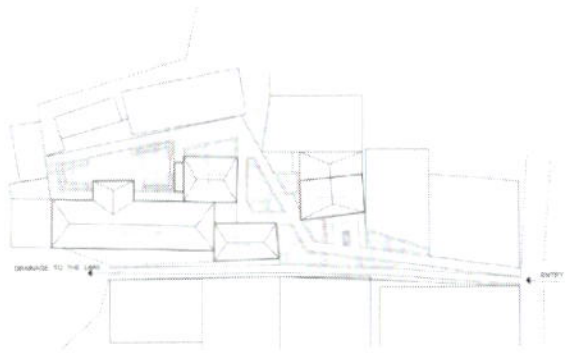

Master plan

JAAGO Foundation School

JAAGO Foundation is a Dhaka-based youth movement, dedicated to improving the socioeconomic conditions of the underprivileged and poverty-stricken people of Bangladesh. The foundation's key goals are battling illiteracy and malnutrition among poor children and helping their families achieve a healthy domestic environment and improved social conditions.

The JAAGO Foundation School, located within the Karail slum—one of Dhaka's largest, at the edge of the upscale Banani/Mohakhali area—seeks to provide high-quality education to the disadvantaged children of this sprawling squatter settlement. With this noble goal, the foundation partnered with Architecture for Humanity–Dhaka, Bangladesh, a local chapter of the non-profit organization founded in the United States, in 1999, to provide pro bono architectural services to distressed and disaster-stricken communities. Together, they created a school with

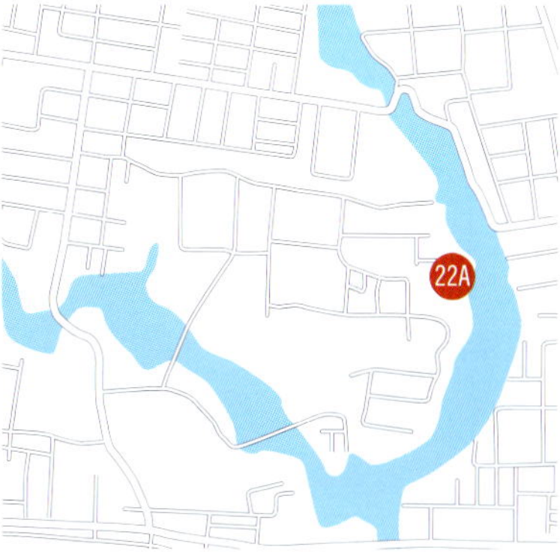

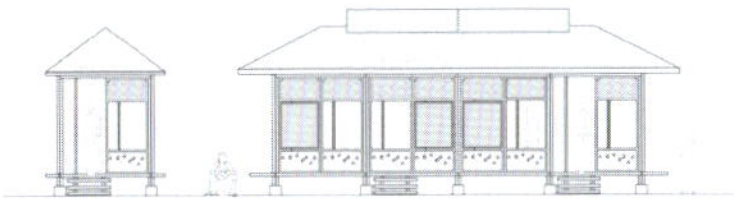

Elevation

cost-effective, prefabricated retractable classrooms.

Led by architect Imrul Kayes and coordinated by architect Rabeya Rahman, the design team conceived of a school building that employs bamboo-panel surfaces and recycled metal structural elements. Abdun Nime served as a landscape designer.
A pervasive building material in rural Bangladesh, bamboo remains underutilized in urban construction, although it is extensively employed as scaffolding, an ephemeral use in the industry. Not only does the JAAGO School create a sustainable learning environment, built with affordable and environmentally friendly materials, but it also champions an untapped market for bamboo: a viable, low-cost alternative to masonry and steel structures.

Built with a paltry budget of US$7,550, the JAAGO School provides an educational facility that also serves as a day-care center. Its modular construction allows for spatial flexibility in a horizontal direction. The school features a well-ventilated classroom, an office, and a toilet, with a combined floor area of 51 sq. m (548 sq. ft.) at a construction cost of approximately US$9 per 0.09 sq. m (1 sq. ft.). In addition to the main structure, there is a community kitchen, an overhead water tank, and a landscaped garden of 93 sq. m (1,000 sq. ft.). It is an architecture of urban grit.

The modest heroism that defines the JAAGO School at Karail is clearly evident in its humility of material selection, cost management, and social mission, rather than in any grand architectural expression. It is a fine example of design as "activism" and the ethos of "design like you give a damn."

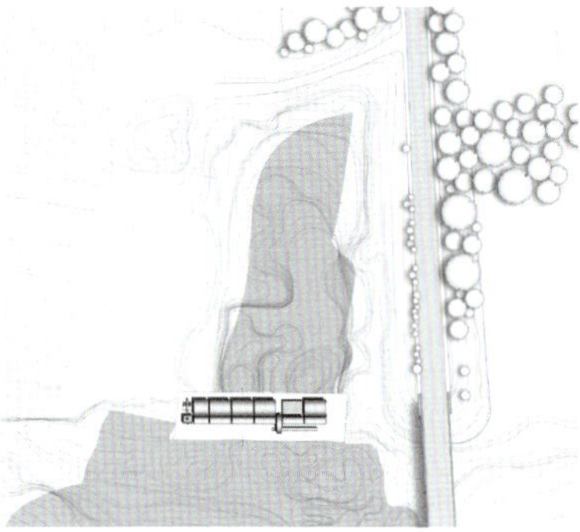

Site with high water level

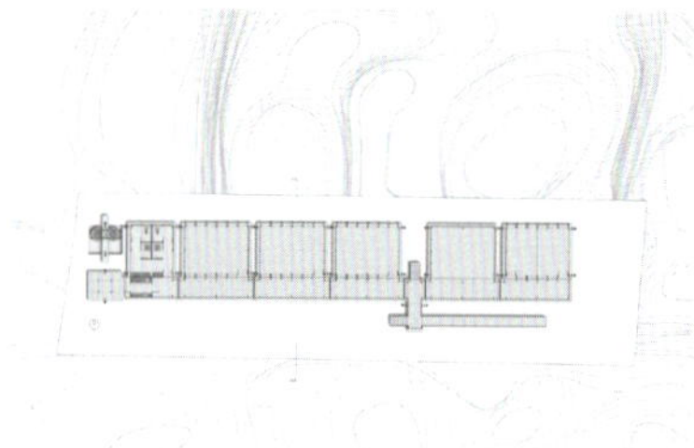

Ground floor plan

Arcadia Education and Vocational Training Project

Maleka Welfare Trust, a Dhaka-based nonprofit organization, has been running a preparatory school for underprivileged children at Savar, north of Dhaka, since 2009. Furthermore, the organization also administers skill-development programs for impoverished mothers so that they can afford their children's continuing education. Both of these programs were consolidated into the Arcadia Education and Vocational Training Project.

The project began its operation in a rented facility, and in 2011, the trust procured a plot of land at Keraniganj, on the bank of Dhaleswari River. The site called for a novel architectural solution because it is located in a floodplain, where water and land coexist, without any permanent borders and levels.

Having received the commission to design the center, architect Saif Ul Haque considered three options. The first was to raise the ground above the typical flood level and build on top of this earthen platform, a com-

Section

mon practice in rural Bangladesh known as "dig and mound." The second was to create a structure on stilts, also a typical form of construction along the water's edge. And, the third was to build an "amphibious" structure—something like a stationary raft—that can settle on land when the water level is low and float when it is high.

The architect pursued the third option. The construction of the lightweight floating structure was completed in 2015. It has a substructure of repurposed steel drums in bamboo framing to facilitate floating. The structure above—including the floor, walls, and roof—is mostly made of bamboo. The building plan is rectilinear, prompted by the shape of the plot. The bamboo edifice comprises five bays, four of which are same-sized rooms. Three function as classrooms in the morning and as training rooms in the afternoon for women from nearby villages. The fourth room is used as an office. The remaining bay functions as an open-to-the-sky courtyard. The center also features a toilet and a pantry at the opposite end of the causeway entrance. A corridor that doubles as a verandah—typical of rural Bengal huts—connects all of the spaces. The curvilinear roof is inspired by the canopies of traditional boats of Bangladesh.

Arcadia Education and Vocational Training Project presents an architecture of sublime spartan simplicity. Its ability to negotiate a pristine geography of land, water, and green reveals how architecture can provide an inspiring learning environment, in harmony with the nature that surrounds it. The project serves as a powerful reminder of how architecture can serve society without muscular self-exhibitionism.

WHEN TO GO

Dhaka's tropical climate primarily features a long wet summer (April to September) and a dry winter (mid-November to mid-February). The hot and humid monsoon season brings nearly 80 percent of the annual average rainfall (185.42 cm or 73 in.).

The best time to travel to Dhaka is during the winter because it typically doesn't rain, and exploring the city is much more pleasurable. The average winter temperature ranges between 12°C (54°F) and 25°C (77°F). It may be a bit foggy in the morning, and the environment may look dusty because of the lack of rain. Although there are fewer hours of daylight, time can be most profitably utilized, given the pleasant weather. The city has much to offer in terms of cultural activities, including art shows, theater, and music festivals, among other attractions. In general, the time around December 16, the country's Liberation Day, is festive.

If travel is not possible during winter, then March and October are also good times to visit Dhaka. The temperature is manageable, and rain is still not a main issue.

It is best to avoid the peak summer months (April to August). Not only does it rain, but it is also oppressively hot and humid: The temperature varies between 25°C (77°F) and 35°C (95°F). However, if this is your only option, there are benefits, too. Longer daylight hours permit more time to tour the city. The bright sun (if it is not raining) provides ample opportunities for taking photographs. Furthermore, after the rain, the city looks fresh and greener! Be sure to pack sunscreen, comfortable shoes, light cotton clothing, sunglasses, and a hat or cap.

HOW TO GO

Air

The best way to travel to Dhaka is to fly into Hazrat Shahjalal International Airport (DAC), about 20 km (12.43 mi.) north of the city center. Getting a visa before the trip is highly recommended. However, upon arrival, a visa is available for a fee, but entails a waiting period. You can buy pre-paid SIM cards for your cell phone, either at the airport or in the city. Grameenphone Service Centers, located across the city, can meet your Internet needs.

It is a good idea to contact your hotel and pre-arrange transportation from the airport. And, once you leave the airport, don't be intimidated by the traffic congestion! It will help to view the streets anthropologically, perhaps, as a quintessential condition of modernity in developing economies.

GETTING AROUND THE CITY

If you are trying to maintain a schedule, take note that public transportation in Dhaka is not very reliable. And, as previously mentioned, traffic is notorious. The best way to maximize a positive experience in the city is to arrange a taxi service through your hotel. A rickshaw is a cheap, zero-carbon mode of transportation. Many consider rickshaws the most effective way of navigating the city. However, there are several thoroughfares that prohibit them. Mini taxis, popularly known as CNGs, are also an affordable way to move from place to place. In all cases, negotiating the fare beforehand is highly recommended.

Many buildings featured in this guidebook are clustered in particular areas. Taking a taxi to visit multiple sites in one neighborhood is helpful. Then, you can walk to the different buildings, although sidewalks can be a challenge. For instance, you can take a taxi to Old Dhaka and walk to Lalbagh Fort complex, the Armenian Church of the Holy Resurrection, and Ahsan Manzil, which are featured in this guidebook. Buildings in the University of Dhaka area/Shahbagh are Curzon Hall, Faculty of Fine Arts, Teacher–Student Center (TSC), the Department of Architecture building at Bangladesh University of Engineering and Technology (BUET), and Priyo Prangan (a multifamily residential complex). And, those in the Parliament area are the National Assembly (Parliament) building, Bangladesh Agricultural Research Council (BARC) headquarters, and Krishibid Institution of Bangladesh (KIB).

THE BASICS

Languages: The national language is Bangla. English is generally understood and spoken with various levels of proficiency. People are typically very friendly and helpful if you have any questions.

Currency: Cash transactions use the Bangladesh taka (BDT). Money exchange locations are available in different areas of the city, including Motijheel, Dhanmondi, and Gulshan.

ATMs: While the majority of the upscale restaurants in town accept credit cards, cash is still the primary mode of exchange. You can find Dutch-Bangla Bank Limited ATMs throughout the city, but predominantly in the Motijheel, Dhanmondi, and Gulshan areas. Most ATMs accept major international credit cards. However, it is easier to withdraw money with a debit card.

Business Hours: It is useful to know the daily schedules for conducting business in Dhaka.

- Government offices and banks: 9 am to 5 pm, Sunday through Thursday.
- Private offices: 10 am to 6 pm; some private banks have special branches that operate from 10 am to 12 pm on Saturday.
- Shopping malls: 10 am to 8 pm; some shopping malls are closed on a particular day. Gulshan and Banani area shopping centers close on Sunday; Dhanmondi and New Market close on Tuesday; and Badda, Bashundhara, and Jamuna Future Park close on Wednesday. (Also see the Markets and Shops, p. 157.)
- Supermarkets: 9 am to 9 pm.

Holidays and Festivals: Friday and Saturday are considered the weekend in Bangladesh. Two major Muslim religious festivals, Eid-ul-Fitr and Eid-ul-Azha, have extended holidays. Dates for both vary, depending on the lunar cycle. Here are some other holidays:

- February 21: Language Movement Day/ Language Martyrs' Day
- March 17: Birthday of the Father of the Nation, Sheikh Mujibur Rahman, popularly known as Bangabandhu
- March 26: Independence Day
- April 14: Bengali New Year
- May 1: May Day/International Labor Day
- August 15: National Mourning Day
- October: Durga Puja (Dates vary. It begins on Shasthi and concludes on Dashami.)
- December 16: Liberation Day
- December 25: Christmas Day

Internet Access: There are many cafés in the Dhanmondi, Gulshan, Banani, and Baridhara areas that offer Wi-Fi hotspots. In particular, Gloria Jean's Coffees, with branches in Dhanmondi and Gulshan, is recommended.

Medical Assistance: In case of a medical emergency, Apollo Hospitals Dhaka can provide a variety of health-care needs. It is a 450-bed multi-disciplinary, tertiary care hospital in Bangladesh.

Apollo Hospitals Dhaka
Plot 81, Block E, Bashundhara Residential Area, Dhaka 1229
Phone: +88-02-84316615
Ambulance: +88-01-714090000 (cell)

Emergency hotline: 10678
URL: www.apollodhaka.com

Public Restrooms: These facilities are available only in shopping malls.

Places to Eat: Dhaka's culinary choices are impressive. Good restaurants can be found throughout the city. However, the best are located in the Dhanmondi, Banani, Gulshan, Baridhara, and Uttara areas. The following website offers various recommendations: www.dhakasnob.com/restaurants_dhaka.htm

Places to Stay: Dhaka offers diverse lodging options. In addition to checking Airbnb (www.airbnb.com), here are some hotels, in alphabetical order.

Amari Dhaka
Bengal Inn
Best Western Maple Leaf Hotel
BRAC Inn
Century Park Residence
FARS Hotel & Resorts
Four Points by Sheraton
Hotel Bengal Blueberry
Hotel de Crystal Crown
Hotel de Crystal Garden
Hotel Dhaka Garden Inn
Hotel Regency
Hotel Sarina
Hotel 71
Lakeshore Banani
Lakeshore Hotel
La Vinci Hotel
Le Meridian
Long Beach Suites Dhaka
Pan Pacific Sonargaon
Platinum Grand
Platinum Suites
Radisson Blu Dhaka Water Garden
Rigs Inn
Rose Wood Residence
Royal Park Residence
Six Seasons Hotel

The Olives Residence & Suite
Tropical Daisy
Washington Hotel
Westin

Markets and Shops: If you are looking for interesting souvenirs from Bangladesh, Aarong (www.aarong.com) is hard to beat! Aranya, Jatra, Jamuna Future Park, Bashundhara, and New Market, among others, are also recommended. (Also see the Shopping malls section, under Business Hours, p. 155.)

Bookstores: Here are three that you may find interesting.

PBS Book Shop
43, Shilpacharjya Joynul Abedin Sharak
(Old 16 Shantinagarl), Dhaka 1217
Phone: +88-02-9345189 or
+88-02-9340530
E-Mail: pbschain@gmail.com
URL: www.pbschain.com

Pathak Shamabesh
204/b (Second Floor), Tejgaon Link Road,
Gulshan, Dhaka
Phone: +88-02-9861003

Shahbagh
Shop No. 17-17A (Ground Floor), Shop 27
(First Floor)
Aziz Super Market, Shahbag, Dhaka
Phone: +88-02-9662766

PRACTICAL INFORMATION

Lalbagh Fort Complex

Summer Season (April to September)
Monday: 2 pm to 6 pm
Tuesday to Saturday: 10 am to 1 pm and 1:30 pm to 6 pm
Friday: 10 am to 12:30 pm and 3 pm to 6 pm
Sunday: Weekly holiday

Winter Season (October to March)
Monday: 1:30 pm to 5 pm
Tuesday to Saturday: 9 am to 1 pm and 1:30 pm to 5 pm
Friday: 9 am to 12:30 pm and 3 pm to 5 pm
Sunday: Weekly Holiday

Goverment Holidays
Lalbagh Fort will remain closed during any government holiday.

Eid Holidays
Lalbagh Fort will remain closed to visitors during Eid day and the previous day of Eid. It will remain open as usual the day after Eid.

Ramadan Holiday
Lalbagh Fort will close at 4 pm during the holy month of Ramadan.

Entry fees

Ahsan Manzil

Summer Season (April to September)
Saturday to Wednesday: 10:30 am to 5:30 pm
Thursday: Weekly holiday
Friday: 3 pm to 7:30 pm

Winter Season (October to March)
Saturday to Wednesday: 9:30 am to 4:30 pm
Thursday: Weekly holiday
Friday: 3 pm to 7:30 pm

Goverment Holidays
Ahsan Manzil will remain closed during any government holiday.

Eid Holidays
Ahsan Manzil will remain closed to visitors during Eid day and the previous day of Eid. It will remain open as usual the day after Eid.

Ramadan Holiday
Ahsan Manzil will close at 4 pm during the holy month of Ramadan.

Entry fees

Museum of Independence

Summer Season (April to September)
Saturday to Wednesday: 10:30 am to 5:30 pm
Thursday: Weekly holiday
Friday: 3 pm to 8 pm

Winter Season (October to March)
Saturday to Wednesday: 9:30 am to 4:30 pm
Thursday: Weekly holiday
Friday: 3 pm to 7:30 pm

Goverment Holidays
Museum will remain closed during any government holiday.

Eid Holidays
Museum will remain closed to visitors during Eid day and the previous day of Eid. It will remain open as usual the day after Eid.

Ramadan Holiday
Museum will close at 4 pm during the holy month of Ramadan.

Entry fees

NATIONAL ASSEMBLY BUILDING (JATIYO SHANGSHAD BHABAN)

It is best to pre-arrange a 4-hour guided tour of the National Assembly building (also known as the Parliament building). You need to bring two copies of the main pages of your passport and visa, along with the Visitor Application Form. You can download the form from this website: www.parliament.gov.bd/index.php/en/visit-parliament

- Hours: 9 am to 5 pm, Sunday through Thursday.
- Fee, paid at the site: BDT 600 per person, payable at the reception area of the Parliament building.
- Fee, paid in advance: BDT 500 per person, payable at the Parliament Branch, Farmgate Branch, or Lalmatia Branch of Sonali Bank.

Contacts:
Pranab Chakraborty
Additional Secretary (IPA)
Bangladesh Parliament Secretariat
Phone: +88-02-8112755 or +88-02-9116120 (office)
Fax: +88-02-8123066
E-Mail: addsec.ipa@parliament.gov.bd

Shawkot Akbor
Assistant Secretary
Visit Branch
Bangladesh Parliament Secretariat
Phone: +88-02-8171323 (office) or +88-01913657476 (cell)
E-Mail: visit.branch@parliament.gov.bd or sakbor83@gmail.com

EXCURSIONS AROUND DHAKA

While visiting Bangladesh, there are wide-ranging, attractive destinations around and beyond Dhaka to consider, as part of your itinerary.

The following two-day trips are highly recommended, not only because they allow visitors to experience life beyond Dhaka, but also because these destinations offer a remarkable diversity of architecture. Given the notorious traffic in Dhaka, trips should be well planned. Visitors should depart early in the day, before the rush-hour traffic begins to swarm the city streets.

DAY TRIPS

Bangladesh Agricultural University at Mymensingh (1965–1975)

Located about 3.2 km (2 mi.) south of the city of Mymensingh (105 km or 65 mi. north of Dhaka), Bangladesh Agricultural University occupies a sprawling campus comprising 485.6 ha (1,200 acres) on the bank of the Old Brahmaputra River. In 1965, the American architect Paul Rudolph (1918–1997) received a commission to create the master plan for the East Pakistan Agricultural University, as it was then called. The university project was part of a building boom that transpired during the 1960s in East Pakistan (now Bangladesh) as a result of a robust American aid package to Pakistan, through such institutions as the USAID, the World Bank, and the Ford Foundation.

The site for the university is fairly linear, bound by the Old Brahmaputra River on the east and by the Dhaka-Mymensingh Highway on the west. Rudolph's approach to the master plan was pragmatic, guided by various climatic considerations, especially building orientation and the concept of the courtyard as a shaded community space. The longer façades typically face north-south, to catch the prevailing breeze. Building plans are highly geometric, forming clusters according to functional type. In many ways, Rudolph's work was modernism with a tropical twist. Before Rudolph arrived in Mymensingh, the Austro-American architect Richard Neutra (1892–1970) had already designed and built a few administrative buildings and the library for the university.

The best way to reach Mymensingh is by a commuter bus or a regional train that departs from the Kamalapur Railway Station.

Sonargaon

Sonargaon (meaning the City of Gold) boasts a range of architectural styles from the Sultanate, Mughal, and colonial periods. Located about 30 km (18.6 mi.) southeast of Dhaka and 6 km (3.7 mi.) east of Narayanganj, Sonargaon was a historic administrative, commercial, and maritime center in Bengal. Medieval Muslim rulers and governors of eastern Bengal made it their seat of government. The village of Mograpara contains a number of historic ruins of Sonargaon, including the single-domed Jalaluddin Fateh Shah mosque and the tombs known as Panch Pir Dargah. Walking about 20 minutes southwest of Mograpara, the visitor will find the tomb of Sultan Ghiyasuddin Azam Shah. The Folk Art Museum and Crafts Village and several early 20th-century houses built by wealthy Hindu merchants should be visited in Panam Nagar.

The best way to reach Sonargaon is to go to Narayanganj first, by a commuter bus or a regional train that departs from the Kamalapur Railway Station. Then, take local transportation to Sonargaon.

MULTIPLE-DAY TRIPS

Sompur Mahavihara, Paharpur

Sompur Mahavihara (the Great Monastery), the largest single Buddist vihara south of the Himalayas, is located at Paharpur in the Noagaon district, in the northwestern part of Bangladesh. With the rise of Mahayana Buddhism in Bengal from the 7th century CE onward, this monastery-city complex became a renowned intellectual center until the 12th century. The vihara, measuring 281.03 m (922 ft.) north-south and 280.11 m (919 ft.) east-west, was declared a UNESCO World Heritage site in 1985. The basic quadrangular layout comprises 177 cells around a soaring pyramidal temple, plus numerous stupas, temples, and other ancillary facilities. Sompur Mahavihara influenced Buddhist architecture as far away as Cambodia.

The best way to reach Paharpur is to take a long-distance bus from Dhaka to the Naogaon district. This trip is approximately 6 hours. Next, board a local bus to Paharpur Bazar, which is about 34 km (21.13 mi.) from Naogaon. From Paharpur Bazar, the site is only a 5 minute walk.

Sundarbans

The largest mangrove forest in the world, the Sundarbans is a vast, river-riddled swamp of shifting tides. The man-eating royal Bengal tiger is one of the key protagonists of this still-untapped wilderness, which is also home to 400 different species of wildlife. It is truly an ecological adventure to remember. According to *Lonely Planet*, even if you don't run into a tiger, "simply sitting on the deck of your boat as you float through thick mangrove forests is an unforgettably dreamy experience." The best way to experience the Sundarbans is to take a boat ride from the southeastern town of Khulna. A day trip may be sufficient, but to truly feel the pulse of this magnificent forest, a three- or four-day excursion is recommended. Travelers eat and sleep in the comfortable vessel, but also have the opportunity to form small groups and take boat rides through river channels (accompanied by armed guards).

The Guide Tours (www.guidetoursbd.com), Bengal Tours (www.bengaltours.com), and Bangladesh Ecotours (www.bangladesheco-tours.com), all of which have offices in Dhaka and Khulna, offer good tour packages. The price per person for a four-day trip can range from around US$200 to US$300.

Cox's Bazar

Cox's Bazar is a beach town, about 161 km (100 mi.) from the southeastern port city of Chittagong. Named after an 18th-century British East India Company captain, it is the resort where Bangladeshis love to go and escape the insanity of city life. Stretching 125 km (77.67 mi.), many Bangladeshis claim that it is the world's longest continual natural beach.

If you would like to relax for a few days near the Bay of Bengal, then Cox's Bazar is an ideal and affordable destination. There are direct daily flights from Dhaka, and three- to five-star hotels are available near the beach.

Modern Education and Training Institute (METI), Handmade School

METI is a primary school located in Rudrapur, Dinajpur, a district in northern Bangladesh, about 320 km (198.84 mi.) from Dhaka. German architect Anna Heringer, along with Eike Roswag, designed the school in 2005. Dipshikha, a local non-governmental organization, initiated the school project with the goal of improving the quality of life in rural areas. This much-acclaimed project used available local building materials and vernacular technologies. And, local craftspeople contributed their skills. The school won the Aga Khan Award for Architecture in 2007.

To visit METI, first take a long-distance bus from Gabtoli bus terminal in Dhaka to Dinajpur. Next, board a local bus to Rudrapur, which is about 20 km (12.43 mi.) from Dinajpur.

Bangabandhu Mausoleum Complex, Tungipara

Tungipara is the birthplace of Sheikh Mujibur Rahman, the father of the nation. Popularly known as Bangabandhu, he was assassinated on August, 15, 1975, along with all of his family members, except for his two daughters. The sprawling mausoleum complex includes the graves of Bangabandhu and his parents; a museum, featuring rare photos of the leader and his family; a library; a mosque; and a cafeteria.

There are two possible long-distance bus routes to Tungipara: One is via Aricha (227 km or 141.05 mi.), and the other is via Mawa (144 km or 89.48 mi.). Both involve taking a ferry across a river.

Shilaidaha Kuthibari, Kushtia

Bengali poet Rabindranath Tagore won a Nobel prize in literature, in 1913, and for more than a decade, he wrote while living in Kushtia. Kuthibari (the mansion) in Shilaidaha, Kushtia, houses the Tagore Memorial Museum, which features a rare collection of photographs, furniture, and memorabilia of Tagore's time here. Debendranath Tagore, father of the Nobel Laureate, built a picturesque three-story bungalow on an estate that comprises 4.45 ha (11 acres) on the south bank of the Padma River, as one of their country houses. Between 1890 and 1901, Tagore wrote some of his masterpieces here, including *Sonar Tori*, *Chitra*, and *Chaitali*. It has been reported that the Padma River influenced the poet so much that he spent most of his time on a houseboat (*bajra*), writing. The Department of Archaeology, Bangladesh Ministry of Cultural Affairs undertook a major renovation of the complex.

Shilaidaha Kuthibari is 15 km (9.32 mi.) from Kushtia. The best way to get there is by a long-distance Kushtia-bound bus from the Gabtoli bus terminal in Dhaka. Next, local transport to Shilaidaha is available in Kushtia.

Shait Gumbad Mosque, Bagerhat

Considered by many to be the most magnificent and the largest brick mosque in Bangladesh, this 15th-century mosque is located in the Bagerhat district, in the southwestern part of Bangladesh, approximately 272 km (169 mi.) from Dhaka. It is a *jami masjid* (congregational mosque), with a vast prayer hall measuring 48.77 m by 57.91 m (160 ft. by 190 ft.). Shait Gumbad mosque means "the mosque with 60 domes." However, the name is misleading; in reality, its roof comprises 77 small domes, including 7 *chau-chala* Bengali domes in the central row. The mosque was declared a UNESCO World Heritage site in 1985.

The best way to reach Bagerhat is to fly to Jessor, which is about 112.65 km (70 mi.) north of Bagerhat. Local transport to Bagerhat is available from the Jessore airport.

INDEX OF ARCHITECTS

BIBLIOGRAPHY

Ahmed, N. (1986). *Buildings of the British Raj in Bangladesh* (J. Sanday, Ed.). Dhaka: The University Press Limited.

Ahmed, N. (1984). *Discover the Monuments of Bangladesh: A Guide to Their History, Location, and Development* (J. Sanday, Ed.). Dhaka: The University Press Limited.

Ahmed, S. U. (1986). *Dhaka: A Study in Urban History and Development.* London: Curzon Press Ltd.

Al-Quaderi, G. G., & Mahmud, A. A. (2010 July). "English Literature at English-Medium Schools of Bangladesh: The Question of Culture." *Pedagogy, Culture & Society*, 18(2), 211–226.

Architecture + Design: A Journal for the Indian Architect (Vol. 4, No. 4). (1998 June).

Ashraf, K. K., & Haque, S. U. (2002). *Sher-e-Bangla Nagar: Louis I. Kahn and the Making of a Capital Complex.* Dhaka: Loka.

Aslanian, S. (2011). *From the Indian Ocean to the Mediterranean: The Global Trade Networks of Armenian Merchants from New Julfa.* Berkeley: University of California Press.

Banglapedia: The National Encyclopedia of Bangladesh (2nd ed.). (2012). Dhaka: Asiatic Society of Bangladesh.

Brownlee, D. H., & De Long, D. G. (1997). *Louis I. Kahn: In the Realm of Architecture.* London: Thames & Hudson Ltd.

Chatterjee, P. (2002). *A Princely Impostor? The Strange and Universal History of the Kumar of Bhawal.* Princeton, NJ: Princeton University Press.

Chaudhury, S. (2011). "The Armenians in Dhaka." In M. M. Islam & F. Mahmud (Eds.), *400 Years of Capital Dhaka and Beyond. Vol. II: Economy and Culture.* Dhaka: Asiatic Society of Bangladesh, 85–94.

Chowdhury, N., & Ahmed, B. (2006). *Mughal Monuments of Bangladesh* (E. Haque, Ed.). Dhaka: An HSBS Production.

Dani, A. H. (1956). *Dacca: A Record of Its Changing Fortunes.* Dacca: The Saogat Press.

Dasgupta, S. (2007). *The Bengal Renaissance: Identity and Creativity from Rammohun Roy to Rabindranath Tagore.* Ranikhet, India: Permanent Black.

Doxiadis, C. A. (1968). *Ekistics: An Introduction to the Science of Human Settlements.* New York: Oxford University Press.

Doxiadis, C. A. (1963). *Architecture in Transition.* London: Hutchinson.

Eaton, R. M. (1996). *The Rise of Islam and the Bengal Frontier, 1204–1760.* Oakland: University of California Press.

Eraly, A. (2007). *The Mughal World: Life in India's Last Golden Age.* New Delhi: Penguin Books.

Frampton, K. (1992). *Modern Architecture: A Critical History* (3rd ed.). London: Thames & Hudson Ltd.

Frampton, K., & Mehrotra, R. (2000). *World Architecture: A Critical Mosaic: 1900–2000, South Asia* (Vol. 8). New York: Springer-Verlag.

Fraser, V. (2000). *Building the New World: Studies in the Modern Architecture of Latin America, 1930–1960.* London: Verso.

GP House: Identity and Representation through Art and Architecture. (n.d.). Dhaka: A GP House Publication.

Griffiths, P. (1985). *Vignettes of India.* Shaftesbury: Blackmore Press.

Haque, E. (1983). *Islamic Art Heritage of Bangladesh.* Dhaka: Bangladesh National Museum, 122.

Hasan, S. M. (1980). *Muslim Monuments of Bangladesh.* Dhaka: Anjuman Printing Press, 54.

Hassan, D. (Ed.). (2008). *Commercial History of Dhaka.* Dhaka: Dhaka Chamber of Commerce and Industry.

Hovannisian, R. G. (Ed.). (1997). *The Armenian People from Ancient to Modern Times* (Vols. I and II). New York: St. Martin's Press.

Hovannisian, R. G., & Myers, D. N. (Eds.). (1999). *Enlightenment and Diaspora: The Armenian and Jewish Cases.* Atlanta, GA: Scholars Press.

Husain, A. B. M. (Ed.). (2007). *Architecture: A History through the Ages.* Dhaka: Asiatic Society of Bangladesh.

Imamuddin, A. H. (Ed.). (1993). *Architectural Conservation, Bangladesh.* Dhaka: Asiatic Society of Bangladesh.

Islam, R. (2013). *Daniel Dunham: Pioneer of Modern Architecture in Bangladesh.* Scottsdale, AZ: Self-Published.

Islam, R. (2010). *The First Faculty of Architecture in Dhaka.* Dhaka: Self-Published.

Kabir, D. S. (2007). *Purbabanglar Railway'r Itihash, 1862–1947 (History of East Bengal Railway).* Dhaka: Probe Printers.

Kali o Kalam (Ink and Pen): *Special Issue on Muzharul Islam.* (2012 September).

Karim, A. (1991). "Origin and Development of Mughal Dhaka." In S. U. Ahmed (Ed.), *Dhaka: Past, Present, Future.* Dhaka: Asiatic Society of Bangladesh.

Karim, A. (1964). *Dacca: The Mughal Capital* (Publication No. 5). Dacca: Asiatic Society of Pakistan.

Kries, M., Eisenbrand, J., & von Moos, S. (Eds.). (2012). *Louis I. Kahn: The Power of Architecture.* Weil Am Rhein: Vitra Design Museum.

Ksiazek, S. (1993). *Changing Symbols of Public Life: Louis Kahn's Religious and Civic Projects (1951–1965) and the Architecture of the Fifties.* Doctoral Dissertation, Columbia University, New York.

Mallick, F. H., & Zainab, F. A. (Eds.). (2012). *Muzharul Islam, Architect.* Dhaka: BRAC University Press.

Mamoon, M. (1993). *Dhaka Smriti-Bismritir Nogori.* Dhaka: Anonnya.

McCarter, R. (2005). *Louis I. Kahn.* New York: Phaidon.

Qaisar, A. J. (1996). *Art and Culture: Endeavours in Interpretation* (Vol. 2; S. P. Verma & M. Habib, Eds.). New Delhi: Abhinav Publications.

Seraj, T. (2011). "Real Estate Developments in Dhaka." In Hafiz, R., & Golam R. A. K. M. (Eds.). *400 Years of Capital Dhaka and Beyond, Vol. III: Urbanization and Urban Development.* Dhaka: Asiatic Society of Bangladesh, 87–102.

Seth, M. J. (1897). *History of the Armenians in India from the Earliest Times to the Present Day.* London: Luzac.

Taifoor, S. M. (1956). *Glimpses of Old Dhaka* (2nd ed.). Dhaka: S. M. Perwez.

Toufiq, U. (1993 January–March). *Sthapottyo o Nirman (Architecture and Construction)*, 18–25.

Vale, L. J. (2008). *Architecture, Power, and National Identity* (2nd ed.). New York: Routledge.

Zahiruddin, S. A., Imamuddin, A. H., & Khan, M. M. (Eds.). (1990). *Contemporary Architecture Bangladesh.* Dhaka: Institute of Architects Bangladesh.

ABOUT THE AUTHORS

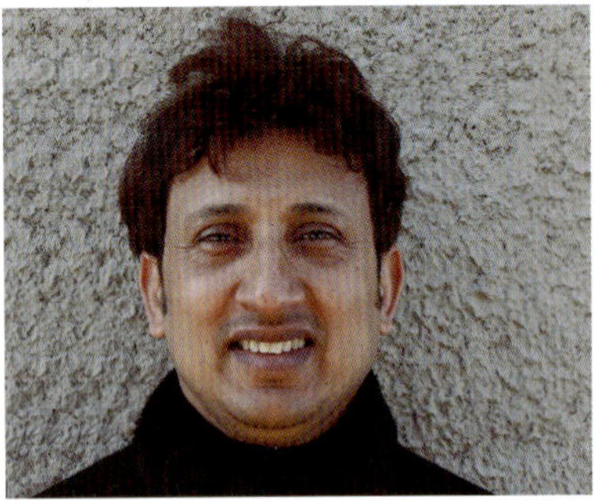

Adnan Morshed

Adnan Morshed received his Doctorate and Master's in Architecture from MIT. Morshed earned his Bachelor's in Architecture from the Bangladesh University of Engineering and Technology (BUET), in Dhaka, where he also taught. Currently, he is an Associate Professor at the School of Architecture and Planning, The Catholic University of America, Washington, DC. In addition, he serves on the Board of the $1M Andrew Mellon Foundation Grant to MIT's Global Architectural History Teaching Collaborative.

Morshed is the author of *Impossible Heights: Skyscrapers, Flight, and the Master Builder* (University Minnesota Press, 2015) and *Oculus: A Decade of Insights into Bangladeshi Affairs* (UPL, 2012). He has served on the Board of Directors of the Society of Architectural Historians, was on the jury for the National Endowment for the Humanities, and, recently, chaired the Society of Architectural Historians' committee for the Alice Davis Hitchcock Book Award.

He has been awarded highly competitive fellowships, including the Wyeth Fellowship at the Center for Advanced Study in the Visual Arts, Washington, DC, and Wolfsonian-Florida International University. And, his research has garnered prestigious grants from, among others, the Graham Foundation and National Endowment for the Humanities.

Morshed has lectured around the world on the history and theory of modern architecture and urbanism and sustainable urban planning in developing countries. In 2012, he led the Society of Architectural Historians' study tour to three South Asian cities: Dhaka, Delhi, and Chandigarh.

His articles have appeared in the *Journal of the Society of Architectural Historians*, *Journal of Architectural Education*, *Journal of South Asian Studies*, *Thresholds* (MIT), *Constructs* (Yale), *New Geographies* (Harvard), *Architectural Design*, and *Traditional Dwellings and Settlements Review*. He has served as a reviewer for various national and international refereed journals and has been cited in various professional and news networks, including *The New York Times* and *Asia News Network*.

A practicing architect and urbanist, Adnan Morshed has designed buildings in the United States, Lebanon, Malaysia, and Bangladesh. He is an avid traveler, photographer, and collector and frequently contributes op-eds to various newspapers and online forums.

Nesfun Nahar

Nesfun Nahar is an architect and urbanist. She began her Doctorate degree research on Architectural Modernism at the Bangladesh University of Engineering and Technology (BUET), in Dhaka, where she is an Assistant Professor in the Department of Architecture. Nahar earned a Master's degree in Housing and Urbanism from the Architectural Association, in London, and a Bachelor's degree in Architecture from BUET. She has been a lecturer at BRAC University's Department of Architecture, also in Dhaka, for 11 years. Nahar took part in various seminars, conferences, and workshops and was a jury member for various student charettes.

ACKNOWLEDGMENTS

Gathering materials on Dhaka's architecture in a timely fashion seemed as monumental a task as trying to chronicle the evolution of this juggernaut of a metropolis in South Asia. Fortunately, many people went out of their way to provide their assistance. I am immensely appreciative of all of those who helped to make this guidebook a reality.

I am grateful to BRAC University Vice Chancellor Saad Andaleeb and Professor Fuad Mallick, who supported this project from the beginning and supplied the lion's share of the research and production costs from the university's coffers. Dean Randall Ott at The Catholic University of America, in Washington, DC, generously covered some of the research expenses and the remuneration of my research assistants.

I would like to thank my co-author Nesfun Nahar, for her remarkable diligence and dogged pursuit of materials that we needed to complete this book. Undaunted by Dhaka's notorious traffic, she traveled from place to place and interviewed all of the contributing architects. How she accomplished this feat, with extraordinary humility, still amazes me.

Special thanks are due Professors Shamsul Wares and Abu Sayeed M. Ahmed of Asia Pacific University, for their initial guidance in choosing the buildings featured in this guidebook. When I first began to work on this project, in Washington, DC, my two research assistants—Emily Pierson and Lillian Heryak—meticulously researched the selected buildings, organized the collected materials, and corresponded with many people, laying the foundation for the book. I could not be more pleased to have had the assistance of these two extraordinarily personable and diligent researchers. Kelly Foley and Sophia Sarver organized the work at various stages.

My sincerest gratitude goes to Robert Boughey, one of the two architects of Kamalapur Railway Station, for sharing his experiences in Dhaka during the 1960s and providing me with vintage drawings and photographs of the station. Turjoy Chowdhury, an accomplished photographer, assumed the critical role of the book's "eye," capturing these familiar edifices from angles that often ricocheted between the creative and the spectacular.

Architects Bashirul Haq, Nahas Ahmed Khalil, Uttam Kumar Saha, Jalal Ahmed, Mustapha Khalid Palash, Rafiq Azam, Ishtiaque Zahir Titas, Iqbal Habib, Salauddin Ahmed Patash, Marina Tabassum, and Patrick D'Rozario provided documentation of their buildings. I owe them special thanks. Kazi Golam Nasir, Chief Architect of the Government of Bangladesh, assisted in retrieving original documents and drawings of the National Martyrs' Memorial. Professors Farida Nilufar and Ishrat Jahan granted permission to photograph the Department of Architecture building at the Bangladesh University of Engineering and Technology (BUET). Rafiqul Islam, a Bangladeshi-American architect based in Arizona, provided valuable information about this building. And, Shirin Iftikhar, Assistant Technical Officer at BUET, submitted a copy of the university's master plan.

I am indebted to architect Nurur Rahman Khan, for his photographs of Shamsul Wares's Kamaluddin Residence. Mohammad Mahiuddin Khan, Additional Secretary, Cabinet Division, Government of Bangladesh, secured permission to photograph Ahsan Manzil. Thanks also to Scholastica School's management, for allowing us to tour the campus in Uttara.

Debashish Roy, of Grameenphone, graciously arranged for us to visit and photograph GP House. Akhtary Begum and Hamidur Rahman, of Bangladesh Chemical Industries Corporation (BCIC), facilitated our photographic documentation of that building. Mostafizur Rahman helped with the photography of Bangladesh Agricultural Research Council (BARC) headquarters.

Architects Khondokar Hasibul Kabir, Atiqur Rahman, Fahmid Ahmed, Faheemul Haq, Tarek Haider, Shamima Muttaqi Annanya, Shawly Samira, Mahbub, and Zishan rendered support in various capacities. A number of architecture students assisted in preparing numerous drawings and documenting buildings. Among them are Sajedul Islam Suvro and Rifat Farzana Shanchari.

Jayson Hait reviewed multiple versions of the manuscript. I can't imagine a more dedicated editorial consultant. Ariadna A. Garreta, of Altrim Publishers, took on this project with a passion. In fact, a few years ago, she requested that I consider writing a guidebook like this when we were navigating Dhaka's congested streets, along with my good friend Franz Ziegler (who graciously allowed us to use some of his Louis Kahn drawings).

This book is a work of love. But, as any author knows, love isn't enough. Love needs help. And, I received it in abundance.

It is an honor to dedicate this book to the Language Movement martyrs who sacrificed their lives on the streets of Dhaka, on February 21, 1952, for the right to speak Bangla.

Adnan Morshed
Washington, DC
January 2017

PICTURES AND DRAWINGS CREDITS

1 Lalbagh Fort Complex
Turjoy Chowdhury
Jalal Ahmad (© J. A. Architects Ltd.), p. 28

Drawings: J. A. Architects Ltd.

2 Armenian Church of the Holy Resurrection
Turjoy Chowdhury

3 Ahsan Manzil
Turjoy Chowdhury

Drawings: Imamuddin, A. H. (Ed.). (1993). *Architectural Conservation, Bangladesh.* Dhaka: Asiatic Society of Bangladesh.

4 Curzon Hall
Turjoy Chowdhury

Drawings: Rifat Farzana Shanchan (based on photograph and plan), p. 45

Haque, S. U., Ahsan, R., & Ashraf, K. K. (Eds.). (1997). *Pundranagar to Sherebanglanagar: Architecture in Bangladesh.* Dhaka: Chetana Sthapatya Unnoyon Society, 44

5 Faculty of Fine Arts
Turjoy Chowdhury

6 Teacher–Student Center (TSC)
Turjoy Chowdhury

7 Kamalapur Railway Station
Turjoy Chowdhury
Robert G. Boughey, p. 64

8 National Assembly Building (Jatiyo Shangshad Bhaban)
Ariadna A. Garreta and Adnan Morshed

Plans and Drawings: Franz Ziegler

9 Department of Architecture Building
Turjoy Chowdhury

Drawings: Department of Architecture, Bangladesh University of Engineering and Technology (BUET)

10 Bangladesh Agricultural Research Council (BARC) Headquarters
Turjoy Chowdhury

Drawings: *Sthapatya o Nirman Magazine* (January–March 1993)

11 National Martyrs' Memorial (Jatiyo Smriti Shoudho)
Turjoy Chowdhury

Drawings: Nesfun Nahar, based on the structural drawing, survey measurement, and photographs. Nesfun Nahar redrew the site plan, from an ammonia copy collected from the Department of Architecture, Ministry of Housing and Public Works, Government of Bangladesh.

12 Bangladesh Chemical Industries Corporation (BCIC) Headquarters
Turjoy Chowdhury

Plans and Drawings: Bashirul Haq (Bashirul Haq & Associates Ltd.)

13A Kamaluddin Residence
N. R. Khan (© Shamsul Wares)

Plans and Drawings: Shamsul Wares

13B S. A. Residence
Daniele Domenicali

Plans and Drawings: Shatotto, architecture for green living (© Rafiq Azam)

13C Karim Residence
Mahfuzul Hasan Rana

Plans and Drawings: Salauddin Ahmed Patash

14 Priyo Prangan Apartment Complex
Turjoy Chowdhury, p. 107
Nandan Architects Ltd. (© Uttam Kumar Saha)

Plans and Drawings: Nandan Architects Ltd. (© Uttam Kumar Saha)

15 Scholastica School
Turjoy Chowdhury
J. A. Architects Ltd. (© Jalal Ahmed), p. 113 (top)

Plans and Drawings: J. A. Architects Ltd. (© Jalal Ahmed)

16 Grameenphone Corporate Headquarters (GP House)
Turjoy Chowdhury

Plans and Drawings: Vistaara Architects (Pvt.) Ltd.

17 BRAC–Aarong Commercial Center
Synthesis Architects

Plans and Drawings: Synthesis Architects

18 Museum of Independence and Independence Monument
Turjoy Chowdhury, pp. 9, 126

Plans and Drawings: Kashef Mahboob Chowdhury and Marina Tabassum

19 Krishibid Institution of Bangladesh (KIB)
Mahfuzul Hasan Rana

Plans and Drawings: Vitti Sthapati Brindo Ltd.

20 Akash Prodip Apartment Building
Nahas Ahmed Khalil and Mahbub Hossain

Plans and Drawings: Nahas Ahmed Khalil and Mahbub Hossain

21 Bait Ur Rouf Mosque
Plans and Drawings: Marina Tabassum

22A JAAGO Foundation School
Architecture for Humanity–Dhaka, Bangladesh

Plans and Drawings: Architecture for Humanity–Dhaka, Bangladesh

22B Arcadia Education and Vocational Training Project
Saif Ul Haque

Plans and Drawings: Saif Ul Haque